Sunset Ideas for
Japanese Gardens

By the Sunset Editorial Staff ■ Book Editor: Jack McDowell

Lane Books · Menlo Park, California

Acknowledgments

The visible delights of a Japanese garden are well depicted in the cover photograph. The garden, located in the San Francisco Bay Area, was constructed entirely with locally available materials. George Murata was the designer; Ken Molino was the discerning photographer.

Drawings used throughout this book to illustrate basic principles are the work of Thomas Creath Watson, who in addition to being an artist is a storehouse of knowledge on things Japanese.

Toshio Saburomaru and the late George Kubota gave much of their time in clarifying esthetic points, as well as a great deal of their energy in demonstrating such practical matters as how to construct a waterfall or how to arrange stepping stones.

A debt of gratitude is owed the many people who made their private gardens available for photographing and who are perhaps the best witnesses of all on the pleasures of owning a Japanese garden.

PHOTOGRAPHERS

WILLIAM APLIN: 65, 104, 157. ERNEST BRAUN: 56, 75, 106 (right). GLENN CHRISTIANSEN: 48 (left), 63 (left), 123 (left), 144 (left). RICHARD DAWSON: 9 (right), 87 (right). MAX ECKERT: 132 (bottom). JEANNETTE GROSSMAN: 63 (right). ART HUPY: 79. TATSUO ISHIMOTO: 6, 10, 22, 84, 92, 94, 96, 99 (right), 125, 141 (bottom right), 154. KASSLER STUDIOS: 62 (right). SAMSON B. KNOLL: 102. ROY KRELL: 61 (right), 69 (bottom left), 107 (left). JACK McDOWELL: 5, 8, 9 (left), 12, 13, 14, 15, 16, 20, 21, 24, 25, 26, 28, 29, 31, 32 (left), 35, 36, 37, 38, 41, 42, 43, 45, 48 (right), 49, 50, 55, 57, 58, 59, 60, 66, 68, 69 (top and bottom right), 70, 77, 80, 83, 85, 86, 87 (left), 88, 89, 91, 93, 97, 98, 99 (left), 106 (left), 107 (right), 109, 111, 112, 113, 114, 116, 117, 118, 120, 121, 123 (right), 127, 128, 129, 130, 132 (top and center), 133, 135, 137 (left), 138, 141 (left and top right), 144 (right), 147, 149, 153, 156, 158. KEN MOLINO: 103. JIM NELSON: 61 (left). DON NORMARK: 32 (right), 34, 61 (center), 101, 152. JOHN ROBINSON: 62 (left). BLAIR STAPP: 33. HUGH N. STRATFORD: 131 (center). DARROW M. WATT: 19, 67, 78, 81, 137 (right), 143, 146, 151, 155. R. WENKAM: 131 (left and right). S. C. WILSON: 69 (top left).

Third Printing January 1969

Contents

Special Features

INVITATION TO ENTER and enjoy American version of a Japanese garden is extended by rustic bridge spanning pond. Garden enhances back portion of a suburban lot in Northern California.

What is a Japanese Garden?

A private corner of nature...a retreat to quiet ... a blend of natural elements... an answer to landscaping problems

The term "Japanese garden" has a different meaning for everyone. Even those who have visited the Orient may retain a mental picture that is an amalgam of anything from raked sand and rocks to wooded hills, moon gates, and rushing water.

Whatever a Japanese garden means to the man who lives in the Western hemisphere, it has for better or worse caught the fancy of many a home owner. From San Francisco to Boston, Japanese gardens have been copied for public parks and corrupted for private residences. Some Americans have spent a good number of hours and dollars duplicating the classical gardens of Japan. Others have been satisfied to paint a Chinese good-luck character in red enamel on their garage door. Though either approach may be in the proper spirit, both can fall short of conveying what is the spirit of the Japanese garden.

The purist may elect to use only the plants

that would be used in Japan. At considerable cost he may import lanterns, basins, stones, and follow the rich philosophy of the traditional garden to the letter. Greater numbers of homeowners, however, are perhaps less interested in carrying out a major landscaping project than they are in finding an easy answer to a weed-choked sideyard that they have been studiously ignoring year after year.

Fortunately, there is a middle ground. Within the framework of good taste you can adapt many of the centuries-old ideas of Japan. Without compromising your desires you can achieve several points common to all Japanese gardens:

You can suggest a closeness to nature.

You can express a quiet and repose.

You can create surroundings that are simple, restrained.

You can beautify an intimate area.

PRIVATE CORNERS OF NATURE

The traditional Japanese garden is designed and constructed according to rigid esthetic principles. Every element has its place, every object, from ground cover to bridge, has a purpose, even if only a symbolic one.

The traditional garden is usually designed on a fairly large scale and is intended as a place for the public enjoyment of various plantings and rock arrangements.

The family garden, on the other hand, is usually a small, intimate area hidden behind walls or fences. It is designed for living rather than display. It is seldom seen by any other than the immediate family and their guests. Most family gardens borrow freely from the classical concepts but they tend away from tradition and toward individual expression.

FAMILY GARDEN IN JAPAN is model of simplicity and a perfect blend of natural and man-made objects. The part of garden shown could serve as guide to planning a natural garden almost anywhere.

. . . IS IT FOR YOU?

The public gardens are a lesson in esthetics. From them you can learn much about making the best use of space, about proportion, about the relationship of structures and garden, about the skillful use of plants, stones, and water. All these are valuable tools in doing something about that awkward sideyard.

IN THINKING ABOUT a Japanese garden that will satisfy your own desires—and in actually planning a garden that you expect to take form—keep in mind three things:

■ *Avoid copying a Japanese garden.* Gardens that you may see illustrated, even in this book, should be considered as points of departure for your own imagination and expression rather than as precise models.

■ *Avoid using plants that do not suit your climate, even though they may be Japanese origin.* Use plants of similar character that will grow in your particular geographical area.

■ *Don't feel that every bit of structural material has to be authentically Japanese.* Imported granite basins and hand-woven fences are fine indeed, but your own part of the country has a great deal to offer in native materials.

A final suggestion might be added: Don't feel that you have to take up the study of Zen or Taoism in order to comprehend what a Japanese garden is all about. Simplicity, understatement, and a feeling for nature are the keys to understanding, and you need no wisdom of the Orient to use them.

If you are a gardener who delights in collecting dozens of varieties of trees, shrubs in all shapes, and riots of flower color, the restraint of a Japanese garden is probably not for you. But if you are happy with the natural feeling of a few rocks and can enjoy two or three types of plants used in harmony, then you are already in the proper frame of mind.

WHAT A GARDEN IS IN JAPAN

One of the outstanding qualities of the Japanese people is their reverence for nature. Since the natural landscape of Japan is made up of rugged mountains, green hillsides, and rocky islands, the main purpose of a garden in that country is to provide a place—in lieu of an escape to the countryside—where a person can retreat for moments of solitude and contemplation. Strictly speaking, a Japanese garden is a representation of the scenery of Japan. Thus, to the purist a Western adaptation of an Eastern landscape is a travesty.

But most Westerners have neither the desire nor the time to immerse themselves in the sea of truth and wash themselves in the stream of Oriental wisdom so they feel less than guilty in enjoying a Japanese *type* of garden in San Diego, or in Phoenix, or in Chicago. The important thing is for you to enjoy a garden on your own terms.

THREE THINGS IN A GARDEN

The special relation of the Japanese garden to nature is a most appealing idea. You observe it in your own garden or a section of your garden when you use plants and other materials to create an abstracted version of something that delights you in the natural world.

Not too many years have passed since gardeners in America thought only in terms of flower beds or large areas alternating in lawn and blossoms. Formal gardens are still a source of pleasure to many who enjoy the kaleidoscopic colors of an English flower garden or the regimented forms of French and Italian landscaping. The carefully planned yet casual appearance of the Japanese garden does not appeal to everyone.

But in many areas of the United States—most notably on the West Coast and the Eastern Seaboard—the idea of the Japanese garden has really taken hold. In some places the appeal seems to be stimulated by the terrain itself. The Pacific Northwest in particular is a place of sculptured landscapes, rich foliage, and abundant water—all reasons enough for natural gardens.

How Much of a Japanese Garden for You?

There are five possible situations regarding your present landscaping. Here are some thoughts on what you might do—or will have to do—in each case to give your site an Oriental touch.

■ *Starting from Bare Ground.* If your site is virgin, the way is open to go as far as you like with a Japanese garden. If you're really serious about it, you'll put in a pond, stream, waterfalls. You'll design major rock groupings. You'll select plants that are the most appropriate. You'll design everything to work together harmoniously.

■ *Changing an Existing Garden.* With established landscaping, you'll have a bit of a job ahead of you to change over to a strong Japanese motif. You'll have to remove some plants, replace others, add new ones. You'll have to modify structures to adapt them to the new theme.

■ *Adding a Partial Japanese Garden.* If you like what you have but want a Japanese garden too, you can landscape a corner or an entry using no more than a previously trained pine, some junipers, bamboo, and a simple accessory such as a stone lantern or water basin arrangement.

■ *Giving Any Garden an Oriental Flavor.* Your touch has to be most subtle here. You can make strong use of space and proportion; create centers of interest with stone, plants, or water; utilize special touches, such as pruning a tree or shrub to display the basic structure.

■ *Doing Something About a Problem Corner.* Is there an area in your present landscaping that you just haven't been able to do anything about? Is it too sunny, too shady, too wet or dry? Is the soil impossible? Give the place some interest and depth by first creating a mound of earth. Use a few large rocks to make an asymmetrical arrangement. If nothing will grow in the ground, try bamboo—it will grow almost anywhere—or set container plants behind the rocks to conceal the pots. If there is enough room without crowding, use a single small lantern.

DIFFERENT TYPES of Japanese gardens, both in California, use plants, rocks to soften man-made objects. Left, tea garden (Design, Shinichi Maesaki); right, moss garden (Design, George Kubota).

. . . BASIC ELEMENTS

Another reason, with special relevance in the eastern states, is the immutability of the Japanese garden. Except for the influence on deciduous plants, strong seasonal changes have little effect on the Japanese garden. It is designed in such a way that bare winter branches have their own particular appeal, and snow becomes a special esthetic element rather than a nuisance. Instead of dead stalks and bare trellises, winter brings to the Japanese garden an added dimension.

Another point of appeal in the Japanese garden is that it does not attempt too much. Rather than make a complete statement, it suggests a point of departure and leaves the rest up to the viewer. Rather than a grand mixture of flowers and shrubs and trees and ornaments it provides a well-integrated series of natural elements, all used with a definite purpose, and all used with restraint—a group of rocks, a simple path, an interesting evergreen tree or shrub. Each part is an object of interest in itself but each has an essential relation with the others. Each part of the garden is in its own way the essence of nature.

Achieving this is not the challenge it may seem. You can capture the essence of mountains with a rock, a stunted pine, and a few river-smoothed stones. You can re-create an alpine meadow with a dwarf fir, some flat rocks, and a small pool. A dozen dark stones scattered over lighter-colored gravel can recall a rushing stream; a five-foot sweep of sand and a low tuft of grass can suggest a seascape.

Whatever the mood of nature you are trying to capture, whatever the landscape you are intending to duplicate, there are three elements that invariably appear in any Japanese garden: stone, plants, water.

Stone is a Natural Framework

It's difficult to imagine a natural garden without stone in some form. In nature, stone occurs almost everywhere in a multitude of shapes and forms. In a Japanese garden, stone is used functionally as well as to assure a natural feeling in the rest of the landscaping.

Stone is used in the garden in many ways. It may edge a pond, line a stream bed, define a walk. It may create a waterfall, simulate a mountain, form a path. A large rock may be used in a clearing by itself solely to create a center of interest, or it may be placed adjacent to an entry for the functional purpose of sitting or stepping.

In Japan, stones are brought many miles to be used in a garden. Commercial suppliers stock not only building stones for walls and paths but keep huge rocks weighing several tons which have

WATER PLAYS MAJOR ROLE in both entry garden at left, which is located in atrium (Design, George Kubota), and pond garden at right, which is cool retreat at rear of home (Design, C. Jacques Hahn).

been brought from remote areas that are known for rock of special form or texture.

The Japanese have even made a special hobby of collecting individual stones that in themselves resemble a natural landscape. *Sui-seki* enthusiasts search for stones with this special appeal and, without modifying their basic form by cutting or chipping, display them much as they would a flower arrangement.

This same love for natural form is apparent in the care the Japanese exercise in choosing and using their garden stone. A stone is more than a piece of rock; it is a design element with a personality and with purpose of its own. Making the most of that personality in the garden is using a stone to its fullest potential.

Plants Bring the Garden Alive

In planning a garden, earth and stone are "sculpted" together first to form a skeleton, a framework with mass that stabilizes the area within itself and in relationship to nearby large forms such as the house. Only after the contours of the land have been arranged, and the rocks and stones placed, are trees, shrubs, ground covers, and other plants considered. Remember this planning rule: stones first, plants second.

There's a practical reason as well. If you're for-

tunate enough to be able to put in a Japanese garden from scratch, starting with bare ground, you'll find that doing the major job of moving and placing rocks beforehand, with no plantings in the way, prevents flattened shrubs and gouged tree trunks.

Planned irregularity, asymmetry, and informality are the keywords in working with plants, as they are with stone. In the Japanese garden there are no straight rows of cedars standing like ramrod-backed soldiers; there are no starkly clipped hedges, looking like pre-cast forms in green concrete. Pines are chosen for irregular form and are trained *not* to look like Christmas trees. Shrubs are planted at angles to the ground and are pruned to prevent their growing into either boxy or ball shapes. The idea is not to cultivate grotesqueness but to encourage the beauty of natural forms.

Generally, evergreen plants should predominate. Pines and firs are the most "Japanese" in character and are used as stabilizing masses.

The Japanese garden is a lesson in asymmetry. When several trees or smaller plants are planted they are generally grouped in odd-number combinations. For example, a planting of nine (rather than eight or ten) azaleas are better arranged in three groups containing one, three, and five plants instead of in precise, regular groups.

Avoid forcing a plant to grow in a situation

IDEAL BLENDING of plants, stone, and water—basic elements of the Japanese garden. Natural-looking stream winds through small city lot, shown in plans on page 154. (Design, Tatsuo Ishimoto.)

. . . PLANTS

that does not agree with its regular environment. A pine whose natural habitat is the mountains should not be used in a simulated seascape.

Deciduous trees should be used sparingly and in the background of a garden, near a wall or fence, where their bare winter branches will form interesting patterns against a contrasting background. An exception would be a blossoming tree, such as almond, plum, or cherry, whose spring display can serve as a point of interest in a central part of the garden.

Here are some principles to follow in your planting if you want to capture the feeling of a Japanese garden:

■ Form the basic plant structure in your garden with evergreens.

■ Give plants space, arranging them in odd-number groupings of similar material.

■ Limit the variety of plantings. The Japanese often plant an entire garden with azaleas, bamboo, and a pine. In a large garden use only three or four kinds of plants. In a small garden use only one or two kinds, plus a single tree.

■ Don't plant annuals in the main garden. If you want cut flowers, grow them in a separate area.

Combine plants and other garden elements according to their associations in nature. Don't mix plants of forests, seashore, and mountain.

■ Enjoy flowering shrubs such as azaleas or Mexican orange for their permanent structure, not just for their flowers.

■ Keep plants in proper proportion and scale by pruning them regularly.

■ Don't overlook the beauty in winter form in deciduous trees and shrubs.

■ Look at fall-colored leaves and spring blossoms as you look at flowers.

Water for Looking and Listening

It takes but a little water to set the mood of a garden. Not all gardens need have a lake or a pond or a rushing torrent of water. A shallow hollow in a basin or mossy rock can hold less than a quart of still water yet give a small garden a certain feeling of freshness. A trickle of water down the face of a rock can produce a musical, refreshing sound and make the surroundings seem cooler.

You can even create the feeling of water where none is available by suggesting a stream bed or dried water course with pebbles, a few rocks, and some ferns.

Pools are relatively easy to construct, since in the Japanese garden they needn't be king-sized. A weekend with pick and shovel, plus a little concrete work, can result in a fair-sized pond; edging it with plants and framing it with well chosen rocks can make it look as if it has always been there.

Water can take many forms in the garden. It can fill a pond, reflect the sky in a basin, bounce along a stream, splash over a falls, or trickle out of a bamboo pipe. Whether it be scenic or utilitarian, real or make-believe, water is almost always found in the Japanese garden.

Even without "live" water you can create a temporary effect by giving foliage and rocks a good sprinkling with the hose. (Sprinkle early in the day, or late in the afternoon, when the bright sun is less apt to burn tender leaves.)

IN PLANNING A GARDEN...

Making a Japanese garden, either from bare ground or from your present landscaping, is not a formidable task. It is a type of garden generally much simpler in its basic structure than most other styles, and the materials you will need are usually fewer.

Remember that the basic elements are stone, plants, and water. Also remember that plants should be limited, whatever the size of the garden, to few varieties. In looking at an area with an eye to turning it into a Japanese garden, see it from the viewpoint of groups of these elements. Try to decide how certain groups could create a scene or a mood or act as a setting for a particular type of garden. Next, depending on whether the terrain is naturally flat or hilly, decide what type of garden will best suit the land and will be the most pleasing to you.

From that point, there are two paths you can take: You can call in an expert, or you can do the job yourself.

Working with a Professional

Landscape architects who are qualified to design and put in a Japanese garden are not as numerous as general landscape architects, but in most large cities there are usually several men who specialize in such work.

Start with the classified section of your telephone directory. Look under "Landscape Architects" or "Landscape Contractors," remembering that an architect helps you design and plan, a contractor helps you build. Often a Japanese name is a fair bet. Some specialists list their qualifications in the advertisement in the phone book. Make a few calls and ask about putting in a Japanese garden. Another phone-book lead is the entry "Nurseries," and again, a Japanese name is a good key. Many retail nurseries may not do landscaping but can refer you to specialists who do.

Landscape architects work in several ways, depending on the job and on your needs. Some expect to work up complete plans, secure bids,

---

✽ What Not to Do in the Japanese Garden

- Don't let bright flowers or large masses of color predominate. Use color mainly for accent.
- Don't use cute plaster figures, quaint signposts, or other out-of-place decorations.
- Don't mix rock forms or rock types that normally do not occur together in nature.
- Don't combine elements that are out of scale with the rest of the garden or with each other.
- Don't use plastic waterfall basins unless they are concealed by earth, rocks, and plantings.

- Don't use colored stones, white gravel, glass, or other non-natural materials.
- Don't arrange garden elements in even-number or equal-size groupings.
- Don't prune trees or shrubs in topiary fashion to resemble animals or man-made structures.
- Don't crowd a garden with every kind of object that has a remotely Oriental feeling.
- Don't paint fences, gates, benches, or other structures; stain them or let them weather.

VIEW FROM HOUSE makes you want to step into garden and spend hours discovering intimate corners. Nandina (heavenly bamboo), brilliant in the sun at right is traditional shrub next to entry.

. . . THE PROFESSIONAL

and supervise the work. Others will work with the do-it-yourself gardener, letting him contribute more of his time.

Most landscape architects charge a consulting fee of at least $25 to talk over your project. If you choose to have one work with you beyond that, his fee may be a lump sum, it may be an hourly rate, or it may be a percentage of the total cost of the project.

The landscape contractor is the man who does the labor of carrying out the landscape plan. He or his crew handle the plantings, install pools, set paths, even build structures. You can have a landscape contractor do all the work, or you can often work with him to keep expenses down.

When You're on Your Own

If you decide to go it on your own, you will derive a great amount of pleasure in planning and re-planning the layout of your garden, then putting the plan into form. You'll feel a closer bond with your garden by knowing that the placement of each shrub and pebble was your idea. In spite of some drudgery—such as spreading gravel— you'll have a sense of achievement and a knowledge that the garden is completely yours from beginning to end.

From the start keep in mind that a Japanese garden is an understatement. It is better to have too little than too much, better to have the garden on the bare side (plants will grow eventually) than overloaded and cluttered.

In Japan a new garden is often a *finished* garden. During construction fully grown trees and shrubs are set directly into the ground, having been supplied by nurseries that specialize in mature plants that have had considerable training for garden use. A new garden looks as if it has been there for several years.

But even in Japan, where labor costs are relatively low, such a garden is an expensive undertaking. In the United States the cost of buying mature plants and of the labor to move them is usually prohibitive. Thus, you must use young plants and be prepared to wait a couple of years for them to fill out bare spots in the garden.

No tree is going to get up in the air to make real shade in less than 2½ to 3 years, unless you spend the money for a specimen size. And the larger the tree to begin with, the more severe you'll have to train it, and the greater the loss

if it doesn't survive. The more patient you can be, the better the garden you'll have in a few years. There's no such thing as an instant garden, unless you can afford it.

How Important is Color?

Generally speaking, the Japanese garden avoids bright colors. If flowers are used, they are grown as isolated centers of interest or for contrast to heighten the effect of some other elements.

A single group of monochromatic blossoms (for example, a clump of deep-orange chrysanthemums) has more meaning in itself and in relation to the rest of the garden than a large bed of varied colors and types. A single tree, or a grove of trees, with bright-hued leaves has more impact than several such trees scattered over a large area.

PUBLIC GARDENS have all the charm and invitation of family garden, only on larger scale. Japanese Tea Garden in San Francisco offers many planning ideas for an intimate home garden.

Many public gardens in the United States are designed entirely in the Japanese tradition or feature a Japanese approach as an important part of their overall plan. Following is a brief survey. Some places charge a nominal admission fee; others are free. See local telephone directories for details.

CALIFORNIA AND HAWAII. Mission Bay, San Diego. Two gardens (Vacation Village Hotel and Murata Pearl Garden at Sea World). Artful use of water, stone, wood bridges.

Guiberson Garden, Bel-Air. Stroll-hillside type with authentic Japanese accessories. Make advance reservation through UCLA Visitor's Center.

Occidental Center, Hill and Olive, Los Angeles. Basement floor features massive rocks, gravel. Roof-top garden has pines, stone, water.

Yamashiro Mountain Palace, Hollywood. Temple architecture, meditation garden court.

Henry E. Huntington Botanical Gardens, San Marino. Plantings, ponds, streams, ceremonial tea house, all on former bare ravine.

Micke Grove Park, Lodi. Pond and stroll type.

Kelley Park, San Jose. Japanese garden covers 6½ acres, includes iris plantings. Completed in 1965.

Hakone Garden, Saratoga. Large waterfall spills into lily pond with islet reached by footbridge.

Central Park, San Mateo. One-acre Japanese garden on east side of park, in the midst of tall, modern buildings. New in 1966.

Golden Gate Park, San Francisco. Japanese Tea Garden is perhaps best known in Western U.S. Tea house, moon bridge, flowering cherries.

East-West Center, Oahu, Hawaii. Japanese garden laid out in form of script character for "love." More than 100 carp in stream.

Honolulu City Hall, Oahu, Hawaii. Dry garden in style of Ryoan-ji, located in atrium.

Lawai-Kai Garden, Koloa, Kauai, Hawaii. Authentic Japanese temple. Private estate, accommodates visitors. Write in advance: John G. Allerton, Koloa, Kauai.

PACIFIC NORTHWEST. Washington Park, Portland, Ore. A 5½ acre Japanese garden with flat garden, sand garden, stroll garden, tea garden. Excellent use of borrowed scenery. New in 1967.

University of Washington Arboretum, Seattle, Wash. Three-acre stroll garden. Large lake with moon viewing platform, ceremonial tea house.

Point Defiance Park, Tacoma, Wash. Tea house, borrowed scenery.

Butchart Gardens, Victoria, B.C. Japanese garden has a lacquered bridge, summerhouses, dwarf trees, and rare blue poppy of Tibet.

Nipobe Memorial Garden, University of British Columbia, Vancouver, B.C. Three-acre stroll and ceremonial tea garden. Tea ceremony arranged for groups of five.

EASTERN UNITED STATES. Brooklyn Botanic Garden, Brooklyn, N.Y. This famous Japanese traditional landscape garden is one of best known in this country. Large *torii* stands in lake, and Shinto shrine is on hill beyond.

Hammond Museum Stroll Gardens, North Salem, N.Y. Pond with stepping stones in "wild geese" pattern.

West Fairmont Park, Philadelphia, Penn. A Japanese garden, and house based on "a 16th . . . century home for a man with leisure for contemplation."

Watson Park, Miami, Fla. Ceremonial teahouse.

THREE PUBLIC JAPANESE GARDENS, each with own special mood. Left: University of Washington, Seattle. Center: Japanese Tea Garden, San Francisco. Right: Huntington Gardens, San Marino.

RED LACQUER BRIDGE *is strong focal point in Japanese Garden at Henry E. Huntington Botanical Gardens. Path and steps beyond lead up slope to house of classical construction.*

The principal color in a Japanese garden should be the green of foliage. Any other colors should be in the natural range—the browns and grays of wood, stone, and earth. Brilliant colors are distracting; earth tones are restful.

THE HOUSE AND GARDEN

The garden—any garden—is a living area. It is an extension of the house, not merely an appendage to the house. The garden should not look like an afterthought, as if it had been stuck on as something to fill up the land around the house. It should flow around and wherever possible into the house.

Sometimes it is difficult to blend a Japanese garden with such architecture as western ranch style or Victorian, but it can be done. It can be done to a limited degree, in such a way that the house will retain its own personality yet will work fittingly with the garden.

Trees Are a Good Answer

One of the best ways to blend house and garden is with trees. Close to the house, use deciduous trees such as maples, dogwood, ginkgo (maiden-hair tree), flowering plum (fruit-bearing trees may be a nuisance if they're too near the house because of fruit drop). If the growth habit is not normally open, prune the trees and train them for an open form; avoid using dense trees close to the house except where you want screening.

Trees near the house should generally reach toward the garden. When you plant a tree you can lean the trunk outward to achieve this. If a tree is already established, you can train its branches in the proper direction.

In planting large numbers of trees think ahead, recalling that they will not always remain the same size they are at the time you put them in. Make sure they have sufficient room for growth without crowding each other or the garden. Some trees—such as birch—are very effective planted in groves, owing to their slim trunks and high, light branching habit.

You can use conifers as long as you don't use too many and keep their forms open, so they won't seem to smother the house. The idea is to be able to view the garden from the house, through the trees, and vice versa. Viewing a garden through branches puts it into a more distant perspective, adding more dimension.

Although some deciduous trees give interesting winter silhouettes against a wall, the evergreens are better the year around for stabilizing

TINY AREA adjacent to swimming pool is small space garden. Screening protects ginkgo from family cat. (Design, F. H. Mick.)

SMALL SPACE garden, with stream running under path, was less than a month old when picture was taken. (Design, T. Itakura.)

ENTRY GARDEN surrounded by brick terrace combines stone lantern, rocks, gravel, bamboo, pine. (Design, George Kubota.)

...TREES

house and garden. Following are some of the more widely used conifers for this purpose:

Pines. Jack pine, Jeffrey pine, Torrey pine, and jelecote pine are all excellent choices for use near the house, since their growth habit is normally open. The popular Monterey pine is a good candidate, as long as you keep it thinned out.

Cedars and Cypress. Atlantic cedar, Hinoki false cypress, golden Hinoki cypress, Sawara false cypress.

Check with your nurseryman or with the *Sunset Western Garden Book* for details on size and growth habits.

In Addition to Trees...

Open-habit shrubs can be used by themselves or in conjunction with trees close to the house. Again, choose types that won't become too dense, or prune them to an open form. Hedge bamboo, a medium-height clumping variety, looks especially good in front of a window, and its stems can be kept thinned out and defoliated near the base for "see through."

You can tie the house in with the garden by running a portion of a pond or a bend of a stream under an *engawa* or deck. Just watch that no wooden structural members of the house remain wet, and allow for at least 6 inches of space between water and deck to avoid the possibility of dry rot. The same result is achieved by continuing gravel areas or ground covers under a deck.

An engawa or veranda links rooms of the house as well as serving as a link to the garden. It makes a horizontal transition between the indoor floors and garden outside. It invites you to step outside. It has the visual property of helping the house achieve an intimate relation to its setting by seeming to divorce its walls from direct contact with the earth. (The engawa is discussed at length in the chapter on useful structures.)

Some other ways of linking house and garden are: running a small open fence (a sleeve fence) out several feet from a wall of the house; using plantings near the house that repeat structural lines of the house; carrying path elements, such as stepping stones, from the garden into the house; using similar plantings inside and outside a large window; painting the house in earthy or foliage colors.

How You Can Borrow Scenery

One of the so-called secrets of Japanese landscaping is that of "borrowing" scenery. If you completely screen off your garden with plants or a fence, it may look like an isolated pocket totally at odds with the surrounding countryside. But when you use plants and rocks and forms within the garden that are also part of the world around your garden, you go a long way toward realizing what is termed organic unity.

If the general terrain around you—or even in the distance—is rocky, use strong, upthrusting rocks in the garden. If your home has a wooded area as a backdrop, try to locate taller trees out at the edges of your property that will visually blend with the distant greenery. If you live in a mountainous area, repeat the hill theme with a mound or simulated mountain in the garden.

If the backdrop of your home is a mixture of roofs and TV antennas, do what you can to "borrow" any trees or greenery in sight.

The idea is to lead the eye from the intimate garden area on out to the surrounding terrain and back again. This has the psychological effect of doing away with boundaries and making even a small garden seem large.

THAT PROBLEM CORNER

An entire Japanese garden may be too much of a project for your involvement. You may like the idea of a Japanese garden but may not want to go all the way. You may have a well landscaped garden that you are satisfied with but still are intrigued with the possibilities of stones, plants, and water used in the Oriental manner. Most likely, you may have only a few square feet to work with—a problem corner that has defied all attempts to make it attractive.

There are a number of special, small-scale gardens based on the Japanese classical theme, but intended for a limited area. Almost all of the ideas and suggestions in this book can be used to enhance virtually any area, regardless of its size or other limitations.

An entry garden is a landscaped area close to the entry of a home, either adjacent to the front door or near it (for example, between the entrance and the street). An entry garden usually must fit a fairly small area and often is surrounded by paving. In such a situation a few bold stones, plus some low plants—juniper, mugho pine, Irish moss, blue fescue—will work well.

If the area will not be overcrowded, you might be able to use a water basin or a single stone lantern as a point of interest in conjunction with plant material.

A side garden may offer a bit more room than an entry garden. The space between an outer wall and the property line or a fence is usually long and narrow. There may be access to it from a bedroom or a bathroom. You can turn such an area into a miniature Japanese garden, a very special place accessible to the room that opens onto it.

Again, keep arrangements uncluttered. A side garden usually cannot take a tree, unless it is slow growing and has an open form. You might create a dry stream bed that winds its way around a small mound and past a group of rocks to disappear into a planting of dwarf bamboo.

A lantern or basin should be small and should be located near a corner or against a wall rather than out in the middle of a side garden.

Even the proverbial corner-where-nothing-will-grow can become a place of beauty. If you can't keep anything alive there—not even one of the hardy bamboos—why not create a dry garden with gravel and a few picturesque rocks.

There is hardly a place on any site that won't benefit by applying some of the ideas of the Japanese garden.

 Books to Help Your Planning

GENERAL SURVEYS OF THE JAPANESE GARDEN

Art of the Japanese Garden, Ishimoto. Crown, New York.
Japanese Gardens, Harada. Branford, Boston.
Japanese Gardens for Today, Engel. Tuttle, Rutland, Vermont.
Landscape Gardening in Japan, Conder. Dover, New York.
Magic of Trees & Stones, Saito & Wada. JPT Book, New York.

USEFUL SUNSET PUBLICATIONS

Decks for Outdoor Living
Garden Pools, Fountains, & Waterfalls
Walks, Walls, & Patio Floors
Basic Gardening Illustrated
Gardening in Containers
Rock Gardens
Sunset Pruning Handbook
Sunset Western Garden Book
Bonsai

STONE IN MANY SHAPES imbues this garden with strength and stability. The beach promontory's lantern symbolizes a lighthouse beside the sea. Note the use of light and dark cobbles set in concrete.

The Stability of Stone

The right garden for you...gaining a feeling for stone...functional stone groupings ...special stones...handling stone

The Japanese garden designer is a master at using stone, plants, and water to create not only a place but a total outlook on life. He brings to a garden plan certain concepts and attitudes. In carrying through the plan he gains new insights, both into nature and himself.

The person interested in the Japanese garden generally is the sort of person who can like and live with the few disciplines it imposes. He appreciates a degree of restraint; he has some feeling for textures and forms; he can see beauty in a single rock.

There are very practical reasons for these things—the restraint, the emphasis on texture and form, the creation of centers of interest, the appeal to the senses. They are important not just for a garden as a garden but also for a garden as an extension of the total living area of a home.

Any area, whether inside or outside the house,

is uninteresting when it has too much in it. It becomes a place that is physically difficult to move around in, therefore tedious or worse yet, depressing. There are many ways to have the things you like without letting them crowd in on you. The trick is to not let yourself be carried away with the over-use of either plants, or rocks, or water to the extent that there is no kind of relief. One attention-getting rock in a garden is special; five (except on a very large property) are ridiculous.

We can learn a great deal from Japanese classical gardens about relating house and landscaping through stone, plants, and water. Though they should be integrated, they should not be tied together so closely—and here is where you exercise restraint—that someone can't tell where one ends and the other begins. Each should retain its personality but the personalities should work together to complement each other.

As shown throughout the pages of this book, there are innumerable ways of creating centers of interest in the garden. Two of them are utilizing texture and form, and using small details. All of the methods can be achieved by using stone by itself or with other elements.

Why a center of interest? What does it do for the total landscaping? A center of interest helps to pull things together—helps to integrate. As an example, if most of the trees in your garden are evergreen conifers, you already have a certain unity, owing to the similarity in textures, color tones, mass. But you'd be hard put to create a center of interest by, say, shaping a black pine in an Oriental manner. It just wouldn't stand out against the similar and competing background. Instead, if you add an element of contrast, perhaps a massive boulder, it will create an island

SEEMING DISARRAY OF STONES is deceiving. Placement took many hours of try-again locating and adjusting to find ideal arrangement for pond and stream. (Design, George Kubota.)

... BLENDING WITH STONE

of interest that will go a long way toward relieving the sameness of the other plantings. Here, a difference in texture, form, and even color create a unifying element.

It's the small details that delight the eye and make a garden an interesting place to be in. It may be something utilitarian as several smooth pebbles at the bottom of a downspout or as prosaic as a stone turtle. These are but two things that create lesser centers of interest but give a garden a human touch.

Too often we tend to think of the garden only as a place to create eye-catching splashes of color or to cultivate the fragrance of flowers. There are other senses to be catered to, such as rough stepping stones under foot or the sound of splashing water. They all do their part in establishing the feeling that a garden is a place for people.

WHAT IS A JAPANESE GARDEN?

In simplest terms a Japanese garden is an asymmetrical yet harmonious collection of stone and plants arranged to simulate a natural landscape. The oldest garden in Japan on record, built around a private home some 1300 years ago, included a pond with a small island, which repeated the feeling of the Asuka River site on which it stood. Stone and plants were taken from the immediate vicinity and structural lines of the garden repeated those of the surrounding area in order that the entire garden would all the more belong in its environment.

The idea of duplicating a landscape by using rocks and other natural materials was by no means an original one that burst into full bloom at that point in time and place. Centuries before, the Chinese had painted and written of such worlds in miniature. And before that, similar ideas of natural landscaping were old in India.

From each culture that has contributed to the development of the natural garden there have come stylistic variations that reflect Hindu cosmology, Chinese Taoism, and Japanese Buddhism. Each has had its own name as well as its own esoteric purpose. The business of classifying things into types is an age-old practice.

Undoubtedly, the first man who ever settled a rock down next to a weed then stepped back to admire his handiwork was brought up short by his neighbor, who wanted to know what *kind* of garden it was. Perhaps the creator mumbled that it was a rock-and-weed garden, whereupon his friend promptly devised a rock-and-weed-and-stick garden, and the science of classifying Japanese gardens was born.

A FEELING FOR STONE

Stone is one of the first elements used in planning and laying out any type of Japanese garden. It forms a strong framework around which the rest of the garden is built. Because of its strength and stability, stone brings a sense of nature wherever it is used.

Stones are the strongest and usually the most dramatic design element in a garden. They can give weight to a fragile appearing architecture and blend together plants and the earth.

ONE LARGE ROCK partially embedded in concrete terrace forms focal point for simple garden at rear of lot. Lantern gives vertical form for contrast. Plantings are azalea, mugho pine.

Stones add strength. They create effects in themselves. They give scale to the scheme in which they are used.

There is a proper balance in the numbers of rocks used. Too many scattered throughout a garden are distracting and disconnected. Too few look as if they were dropped around accidentally and tend to be overpowered by other garden elements.

Overpowering one element with another should be avoided. No Japanese garden should be all stone (an exception would be the Zen sand garden), nor should it be all greenery. The trick is to find the proper balance between both and thus enhance each.

Avoid regular forms. In nature a perfectly round stone is a freak. It is the irregular shapes and variety of surfaces on stone that give a rock character. Also, in groups of stones avoid using several of the same general shape or size. Differences in mass and form make a composition alive and appealing.

Even numbers of stone in proximity are static. Two, or four, or six stones together are complete, and tend to cancel each other. Odd-number groups balance in their asymmetry and the unequalness attracts the eye.

The Japanese see a higher meaning in stones. To them stones are eternal, never changing. They

WITHOUT THE ROCKS, transition from house to garden would be too abrupt. Large rocks edge small area (only 12 by 14 feet) but also stabilize garden with floor level. Rough-hewn well on left.

 **Five Basic Stone Forms**

LOW, ROUNDED FORM

This form resembles a fairly smooth mound with sides that angle out broadly at the base, blending it solidly with the earth. Its shape is peaceful and gentle in feeling. Use singly or in groups to simulate low mountains or hills. Situate slightly above eye level to give stability to the form and the illusion of greater mass.

TALL, RUGGED FORM

This type of rock is two or three times taller than it is wide, looking like a peak that has been pushed up, out of the earth. The basic shape is disruptive and exciting. Use several rocks of this form in constructing waterfalls. Combine rocks of this form with low rocks to create a mountain group containing steep cliffs and rounded hills. This form can sit vertically or can lean slightly but should always lean in toward the center of a grouping. Tall rocks must be well stabilized in the earth or they will appear to be toppling over.

IRREGULAR FORM

This type of rock is much less symmetrical than either the low or tall form. Its base should usually be broader than its top, to avoid a feeling of imbalance, but hollows and slight over-hangs are often attractive. Its strength is in its asymmetry. Use this form to provide a solid counterpoint or balance for any other form, or use a large boulder of this form by itself for a center of interest.

PROSTRATE FORM

This form is two to three times as broad as it is high, and its top is irregular with low peaks and shallow hollows. Because of its low mass it has a feeling of permanency. Use the prostrate form in conjunction with water (or gravel in a dry garden) to simulate low islands or land forms along the shore.

FLAT FORM

Here is the classical stepping stone—broad and flat-topped. It is stable and peaceful in feeling. Use this form for paths (settle it firmly), for a "display" stone (base for a lantern or bonsai), for a shoe-removal stone, or for a simulated boat landing at the edge of a pond.

HERE IS STONE *just as you see it in garden supply centers. Lace rock, both pictures on left, comes in variety of sizes. Gravel bins permit wide selection of smooth stones.*

. . . MEANING OF STONES

imply strength and symbolize a constancy that outlives all else.

The placement and form of stones traditionally have had great symbolic meaning to the Japanese. Certain tall stones suggest tall mountains; pointed stones suggest fire; low, flat stones symbolize gentle hills or calm water. In addition to their natural symbolism, stones can imply definite moods. Sharp, jagged forms convey a feeling of discontent, whereas smooth stones generally convey repose and peace.

Spiritual symbolism is much more charged, much more dependent on a rich culture of Hinduism and Buddhism. The "celestial ship stone" is a good example. In Japanese mythology one of the gods loaded a ship with precious jewels and descended to earth. The celestial ship has thus become the subject of numerous plays and stories and, perhaps owing to its happy theme, is often represented in gardens. (There is a celestial ship stone in the Japanese Tea Garden in San Francisco's Golden Gate Park. As you descend the very steep flight of concrete steps whose top is

surmounted by the large wooden arch, look to your right. Where the cascading water enters the pond snug against the hillside, a celestial ship appears to be sailing toward the falls.)

Stones may suggest, in their form, a turtle or a crane, both of which in turn stand for long life. A stone may resemble the conical shape of Japan's Mount Fuji, symbol of the eternal.

It is evident that in a Japanese garden stones do a great deal more than serving as places to step. In almost every photo in this book you will find rocks in one form or another, attesting to the feeling for stone in the Japanese garden.

WHICH GARDEN FOR YOU?

Depending on the book you go to, you are apt to find Japanese gardens categorized in any or several of three to two-dozen ways. Most of them boil down to the large garden or the small garden. Most public gardens are of the large, stroll type, meant for the enjoyment of numbers of people. The small family garden is more intimate and is

FOUR MASSIVE ROCKS and moss-covered mound create very special place. Nearly half of each rock is buried in earth to stabilize mass. (Design, George Kubota.)

connected to a residence. This book treats five types of family gardens, each distinct by virtue of its size, its use of stone and other materials, or its purpose. These are:

Tea garden,
Hill garden,
Flat garden,
Passage garden,
Sand garden.

A sixth catch-all category covers such combinations as the small-space garden, the indoor garden, and the rooftop garden.

The Tea Garden

The tea garden requires considerable space since traditionally it consists of an outer and an inner garden. It includes a structure—a tea house. The tea garden is perhaps the most charming but the most elaborate. It requires at least 600 square feet of space, and almost always—owing to its intimate nature—it must be enclosed for privacy.

The outer garden forms a buffer, to shield the tea house from the noise and confusion of the world. The outer garden is a comparatively narrow space with a stone path that leads through a gate to the inner garden, then to the tea house. Alongside the path there is usually a stone lantern to light the way. The outer garden has simple plantings and stone groupings.

The inner garden is a small, subdued area adjacent to the tea house, containing a few plantings, some rocks, and a water basin grouping.

Historically, this type of garden was intended as a place where persons were invited to partake of tea and wherein all worldly cares and troubles were for the short period of the tea ceremony put aside. Within the garden, and especially within the tea house, all men became equal and could enjoy the sight of a leaf that had fallen on the path or the sound of water coming to a gentle boil in an iron kettle, no matter what their rank in life.

The Hill Garden

The hill garden is considered by many enthusiasts as the ideal garden. It uses changes in level and stone to represent a mountainous landscape on a miniature scale, giving the impression of a large area of countryside.

A hill garden can be designed for an area of

almost any size since it makes use of perspective to maintain a reduced scale. Some of the most charming gardens of this type have been built in a restricted space just outside a window. Though such a garden may encompass no more than 15 square feet, it can give the illusion of a landscape several miles in extent.

Hill gardens have one or more hills formed with earth mounds and exposed stones. Sometimes this type of garden has a pond as well as a stream and a waterfall. If water is impractical, its presence is hinted at by means of a dry stream bed or dry shoreline.

Of course, the smaller the actual area, the smaller must be the elements in it to maintain the proper scale. Use can be made of small trees —especially in the background—that are pruned and trained in such a way as to restrict their full growth. Any ornaments—such as lanterns or pagodas—must be in perfect scale or they will destroy the illusion of a real landscape.

The Flat Garden

The flat garden pretends to be a mountain valley or an open meadowland. It can be on a relatively small scale encompassing an area of no more than 100 square feet. A flat garden is not necessarily pancake-flat; it may simulate low, rounded hills by using stones, earth mounds, or a combination of both.

The flat garden is designed to be looked down into. Large rocks are chosen and arranged to lie close to the earth, and plants are trained to spread close to the ground. Strong vertical lines—as created by tall pines or birch trees—are avoided since these counteract the restful feeling of smooth, low planes.

The Passage Garden

The passage garden is a most useful landscaping device for a narrow area, such as the space between two houses or between the outer wall of a home and a nearby fence. Since such areas are often confined, their landscaping must be simple to avoid a crowded or cluttered appearance.

FLAT GARDEN simulates shallow valley with lake and streams, draws the eye on through its length. The irregular shore, earth mounds, rocks, and plantings give interest and perspective to the entire area.

Seldom should lanterns, pagodas, basins, or other man-made accessories be used in a passage garden. Instead, it should contain a few key stones, all of them in scale, plus two or three types of plants which complement each other and their surroundings in size and shape.

Avoid using bushy trees and shrubs in a passage garden. Instead, choose plants with open forms and slender shapes.

Paths should be simple. If water is desired, it should be the merest trickle over a rock.

The Sand Garden

The traditional sand garden is extremely simple. It uses stone and little else. One of the best examples of this style of landscaping in Japan is the Ryoan-ji garden in Kyoto.

The Ryoan-ji garden is a rectangular area of about 360 square yards adjoining a Zen Buddhist temple. It contains fifteen rocks arranged in five groups, space between being filled with fine, white gravel raked in simple patterns. There are no trees or shrubs, only moss growing at the base of some of the rocks.

The garden is a statement in simplicity and beauty. As one writer has said, it is symbolic but the interpretation of its symbol depends on the individual.

The flat sand garden is usually not to the liking of Americans, at least on a large scale. Its simplicity can seem stark to those who like a wealth of plant material, and it must be attended to often to keep it at its best. This type of garden can be effective and pleasant if confined to a small area, such as an entry or indoors.

Indoor Gardens and Rooftops

Any of the foregoing small space gardens can be used as an indoor garden, assuming that you choose plant materials that will survive inside the house. In lieu of a natural ground cover, use a layer of gravel. To keep from having to wrestle large stones into the house, use light feather rock.

You can hide plant containers behind rocks and partially conceal large containers with the foliage of low plants. As with any potted plant indoors, use a drainage dish under each container and in addition put a waterproof plate or lid under the drainage dish to prevent moisture from mildewing the floor.

The purpose of an indoor garden is to bring natural scenery indoors. If an indoor garden can be near a large, low window, on the other side of which are outdoor plantings, the garden seems to be both inside and outside and the glass seems hardly to exist.

THREE LARGE SLABS of flagstone form sturdy, natural bench for garden. A place to sit invites you to linger and enjoy surroundings. The path is made of same kind of stone as bench.

. . . INDOOR GARDENS

You can eliminate decisions on plant choice and care by using only rocks and gravel. To help the natural look, cut various lengths of large bamboo from six inches to a foot and stand them upright to resemble pilings. Or, you might want to carefully wedge lengths of bamboo between ceiling and floor to give the impression that the bamboo is growing indoors. Don't arrange all the lengths perfectly vertical but, as in nature, have them seem to arise from a common area and grow out in diverging directions.

See page 131 for more suggestions on bringing the garden indoors.

Since size is a factor indoors, the sand garden often can be effective. A flat garden will sometimes work well, and a hill garden—if kept on a small scale—can give the illusion of a larger area. Whatever type of garden you adapt for a small space, don't attempt to liven it up by adding quaint miniature bridges, toy lanterns, or statu-ettes. They will spoil the entire effect and make the place look like a gee-gaw collection rather than an understatement of nature.

Some homeowners have constructed small space gardens on a deck or terrace or even on a rooftop. In such places the garden should be separated from wooden surfaces by several thicknesses of tarred builder's felt. If you're thinking of this kind of scheme, you would be well advised to have a contractor check the roof area to make sure it will stand the weight of a garden plus that of a person or two.

NATURE'S WAY IS BEST

Fortunate—at least from the viewpoint of the natural garden—is the man who lives on a naturally stony site. If you have access to places where stone thrusts up out of the earth or lies in great masses on the ground, take some time to observe the way nature arranges things.

A few minutes of looking around the next time you are hiking in the mountains or lazing at the beach will help you to understand the natural occurrences of stone. Especially pay attention to the subtle ways that earth and stone and plants exist in a marvelous visual balance that man can only strive to duplicate.

The aim in arranging stones in an artificial landscape is to make them look as they would if they had been placed there by nature. Even a seemingly regular arrangement of stepping stones can be made to look natural. A good way to gain a feeling for stone placement is to play around with a small-scale model. Use a tray landscape to arrange pebbles and small rocks to see how they work together and fit into a "best" relationship with each other and the surface beneath them.

FUNCTIONAL STONE GROUPS

There may be a situation in which you will want to use a single large rock as a center of interest in a garden. Individual rocks have a character of their own, as discussed later under proportion and balance. It is this character that makes a certain rock the only "right" one for a particular situation. Usually a rock must also work with other rocks, must complement them and be complemented in turn. Thus, rocks must be considered from two standpoints: their individual character, and their ability to work with other stones.

Stones that Add Height

Tall, vertical-form stones are used to give a feeling of height. Such stones are somewhat conical in shape and are significantly taller than they are broad. A single tall stone (some Japanese refer to them as "statue" stones), when properly placed, looks as if it had been thrust suddenly out of the earth. A tall stone by itself, or several tall stones together, convey a strong feeling of sudden-ness . . . of excitement.

A tall stone accompanied by several low-form stones tends to be subdued. Its vertical strength is tempered and in effect it is brought closer to the earth.

If you want a feeling of real height in a garden, use a tall stone either by itself or with other tall stones near the top of an earth mound. A stone even three feet in height will have a certain magnificence when situated on a low rise of ground. The taller the form, the stronger will be this feeling to a viewer.

Use a group of tall stones in a low or level area if you want to break up the impression of flatness.

ROOFTOP GARDEN in commercial building has moss-covered basin nestled in smooth, black stones. (Design, Eljiro Nunokawa.)

SERIES OF LARGE ROCKS along path, with plantings of juniper, pine, separate adjoining properties. (Design, George Kubota.)

ONE LARGE ROCK with flat top helps create raised bed for pine, flowers, separated from lawn. (Design, Frank Shinoda.)

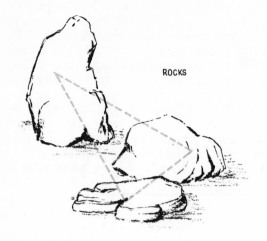

ROCKS

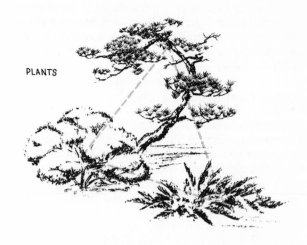

PLANTS

BASIC TRIANGLE is ideal design guide, whether used with plants, rocks, or both. Regular triangle—all sides equal—makes groupings too stilted; strive for asymmetry of unequal-sided form.

. . . USE OF STONE

In using tall stones, watch that surrounding elements are not all of similar form unless you definitely desire an overwhelming vertical design. For example, a tall stone backed up with bare bamboo stems in front of a stake fence will result in all up-and-down lines. Too much of this can make you feel that you're behind bars.

On the other hand, don't weaken the character of a tall stone by surrounding it with too many low elements. A tall stone in a flat area creates a strong and pleasing contrast; if the same stone is also swamped with miscellaneous rocks and low-mounding shrubs, it will visually become just a formless object.

Tall stones suggest cliffs and mountain peaks. With other forms, they can create a simulated waterfall or make up a real one.

If you want contrast, use tall forms against flat forms. If you want height, use tall forms by themselves on a rise of ground.

Stones to Use in Low Areas

Low stones have a prostrate form. They are horizontal rather than vertical. They mound somewhat on top but only enough to make them impractical as stepping stones. Low stones are shaped somewhat like a turtle's back. When placed properly they should seem to hug the earth and be more an integral part of it than does a tall stone.

A low stone should not have perfectly vertical sides (as flagstone does). Its general appearance should be that of a gently mounded hill rising from the earth.

Low stones are stable. The larger they are—that is, the wider they spread out in relation to their height—the more massive and comfortable they seem. When a low stone is well-settled in soil and moss, or if a ground cover has grown to conceal its edges, it appears to be a permanent part of the earth. (Be sure to keep ground covers from completely taking over a low stone. Let enough growth just hide the edges and form an irregular pattern without inundating the entire rock.) Several branches of a low-growing plant—such as *Juniperus horizontalis*—reaching out over a low stone will help to soften its form.

In a sand garden or in a pond a low stone can look like an island.

Low forms should be used carefully, since they can easily be overpowered by nearby strong elements. A large low stone can often be used next to a tall lantern or pagoda. The lines of each tend to balance the other and to blend both into a harmonious grouping.

Three low stones of different sizes can be located to good effect on the side of a slope. They serve no practical purpose but tend to direct the eye on up to the top of the mound, where you might locate a lantern, a bonsai, or a grouping of tall stones.

Several low stones can be used along the edge of a pond to symbolize a seashore. A long stone helps to divide land or water into pleasing areas.

In placing several low stones in a group, vary their height and use different-sized rocks so they don't look like stepping stones.

Stone Can be an Island

Many natural rocks fit neither into the tall nor low category. Some have a rounded form and are almost spherical. The danger in placing stones of this form directly on the ground is that they look as if they had rolled there.

All stones should fit into the ground rather than sit on it. This is especially important with round stones. If they are not embraced by the earth, they appear to be moving.

Round stones are used to simulate hills or low, gentle mountains. They can also be used in water to suggest steep-sided islands. Several of them arranged in a gentle curve will be reminiscent of Japan's island chains. Round stones that are sunk deep into the earth can be used in odd-number groups merely as ornamentation. Singly or together they give a quiet, full feeling to an area. They are not as peaceful as low stones but much more restful than tall stones.

Small round stones (4 to 6 inches in diameter) can be used to edge a pond or a path. Don't be too precise in placing such a rock edging or it will be obviously man-made. Use rocks of various sizes (though not widely different in size); set some of them more deeply into the earth than others; avoid straight line-ups; and don't fill the spaces between with smaller pebbles.

A tall stone lantern can be balanced nicely with three or five round stones. A round stone near the base of a straight tree with a long trunk (such as birch or high-pruned pines) helps to offset the strong vertical trunk line.

Water basins are often made by hollowing out a depression in a round stone. Round stones are sometimes used for a low retaining wall, since they form a more pleasing surface than a wall made with cut or flat rocks.

LARGER ISLAND, at upper right, and promontory are formed by rocks and soil, support growth of shrubs, small trees. Rock jutting out of pond makes disconnected element, but one that belongs.

CHOOSE YOUR OWN garden stone, to get rocks that will fit into the overall plan. Two men with truck-mounted hoist can position and place large flagstone (see at left) or good-sized rock.

... TYPES OF STONES

If a round stone isn't too small, you can sometimes set a lantern on it. Make sure that the rock has more mass than the lantern or the effect will be one of imbalance.

IF A ROCK isn't tall and isn't low and isn't round, what is it?

It's irregular.

Irregular stones have strong planes and deep indentations. They are used to provide a stable counterpoint for other forms.

Some irregular stones are used for their own form, such as the celestial ship stone—which is supposed to resemble a ship under full sail. Irregular stones are often used in ponds or in streams to create eddies in the water. Beware of using rocks that look like eggs or animals. Such sculptures don't belong in a Japanese garden.

Stones for You to Walk On

Of all stone forms, the flat stone is perhaps the most stable and peaceful. Flat stones are used chiefly for stepping stones, for paving, and for garden steps. They may be anywhere from an inch to a foot or more in height.

In some of the early Japanese gardens, paths were surfaced with sand or were merely compacted earth kept free of weeds and pebbles. Sand was too difficult to walk on, and beaten earth would receive too much abuse from *geta*, the Japanese wooden clogs. A logical answer, and one which also kept feet away from wet soil, was stepping stones.

In designing a path, flat stones in irregular shapes are laid out in step patterns—one stone per step—or arranged tightly for a paved path. Regular-shaped flat stones are usually arranged as paving. (Details on stone paths are given in the chapter on walks and paths.)

Flat stones are always used for stepping stones; other uses are fairly specialized. A flat stone can serve as a base for a lantern and it can be used for a bench. Large flat stones, either cut or with a natural shape, are used for foot bridges. Several flat stones play an important part in the classical water basin grouping.

If a flat stone is to lie in its normal flat position, it should fit into the earth and not look as if it had been dropped on the ground. Plant a low, spreading ground cover around and between flat stones (Irish moss, Scotch moss, baby's tears) and let it spread around the edges of the rocks but not overgrow them.

Flat stones are occasionally used as foundation stones for decks, engawas, roof supports, and dock pilings. Most building codes in the United States do not allow stone for even limited foundation use, though the effect can be achieved by setting a rock in the concrete used for foundation, then resting a vertical wooden member on the stone.

WORKING WITH STONE

Few people own property with enough natural stone on it to use for a garden, and there are few places in the wild where you can freely gather rocks. Some areas have laws that prohibit removing stone or even sand from public beaches, and offenders can be subject to a stiff fine for violating them.

Unless you have open and lawful access to natural stone, you'll have to order your materials from a supplier. Look under "Rock," or "Stone," or "Garden Materials" in the classified section of your phone book.

Some suppliers will let you choose individual rocks, which is to your advantage. You know, or you should know, what forms and generally what sizes you'll need, and you can't expect the supplier to take the time to pick over a pile of stone to find just the right ones.

In planning your stone arrangements, and later

 How to Grow Plants in a Rock

The picture sequence below shows how you can use one type of natural rock for a plant container. In the proper setting—partially buried in the soil, or in the company of other rocks—the arrangement has a natural look that no container plant could approach.

The rock illustrated is coarse pumice, found in many volcanic areas throughout the western United States or usually available from stone yards. Choose a handsomely shaped piece, the larger the better; it's so lightweight you'll have little trou-

ble moving it into place. Gouge out holes, fill them with a soil mix having good drainage (1 part coarse sand, 2 parts fertile garden loam), and grow plants right in the rock.

The plant's roots will eventually work down from the pockets of soil into the tiny hollow channels in the rock. The whole rock is like a giant sieve, so drainage is perfect for alpines or azaleas.

Water the entire rock daily. Feed occasionally with a liquid fertilizer. In a shady location, moss will develop.

LEVEL BOTTOM of pumice rock with old ax, then alter shape by chipping carefully with ax or chisel. Newly cut surfaces are same color as weathered rock. Maple stays small because roots are confined.

SMOOTH COBBLES around tree make good transition between grass, large stones, water. The oversized gravel looks almost like stream winding to the lake. (Design, Laurence Korsmos.)

. . . THE BEST STONES

in choosing the rocks, think in terms of "families" of stone. Although an entire garden needn't use only one kind of stone, don't create a hodgepodge by using several different kinds and forms. If you like the appearance of, say, black granite, then use enough of it that its presence in the garden won't seem like a rare occurrence.

Be cautious about mixing together two or more types of stone (such as granite and sandstone), or using smooth stones along with sharp-edged stones. Try to keep at least individual groupings restricted to one kind of rock.

The most desirable rocks are those covered with moss or lichen, such as the type called field stone. When you see such rocks in the supply yards they may look dry and crusty but once they receive a little moisture their covering turns a rich, lush green.

To retain the natural look in every way possible, avoid using rocks with bright colors, unless they are actually a type of stone native to your area. Usually, the earthy browns and grays are the best natural stone colors. Dolomite is a brilliant white rock, commonly sold as a coarse gravel for beds and ground cover. Though it has its place in certain landscaping, dolomite is usually too glaring and artificial looking to be used in a Japanese garden.

Every rock has a back and a front. The front is the part that looks the best. If the front of a rock has a defect, such as a deep scratch, you can sometimes hide it with foliage.

Here are a few guides to selecting and working with stone:

■ The size of the stone you use sets the scale for your garden; other elements—such as plantings, lanterns—must fit the scale of the stone work.
■ Rocks must be in good proportion to each other as well as to the entire garden.
■ As a general rule, use small stones in small gardens, large stones in large gardens.

Consider Proportion and Balance

A rock that is larger at its top than at its bottom is difficult to balance visually. Unless you sink it deeply into the earth its overhang will make it seem to be teetering for a fall.

Rocks of generally the same form (low, or tall, or flat) usually work well together. Also, rocks that balance each other in size, shape, and location give a total balance to a grouping.

Avoid using extremely large and extremely small rocks together. The small ones will be overpowered and look ridiculous. Don't use several rocks all of the same size or height, but on the other hand avoid random sizes. Instead, choose sizes and arrange them to form a progression from small to large, or vice versa.

In a grouping of rocks try the effect of using a single form that is different from its neighbors. With a series of round stones you might locate a sharp-edged form for contrast. Sometimes this works, sometimes it doesn't. If the arrangement just doesn't seem right, then take out the foreigner and stick to all similar shapes.

When you set out rocks, plan their spacing carefully. If you take a handful of pebbles and drop them on a surface, you'll note how randomly they tend to be spaced. Seldom will all of them have precisely the same space between. There will be clusters of two or three or more, and the clusters will have odd spacings between them. Aim for this natural effect in arranging large rocks in the garden. Make small groups within larger groups, each with a pleasant pattern of spacing.

A first arrangement may look good to you close up but when you step back and inspect the grouping from several angles you may find that several rocks in it are in a perfectly straight line. It may be a frustrating job to manhandle the stone over and over again to attain the one "perfect" arrangement but the end result is usually worth the effort.

SMOOTH COBBLES are traditional Japanese way of creating beach. In the large pond they needn't cover entire bottom.

Arranging Garden Stones

If there are lines of stratification on rocks that you plan to use, try to make all of the lines go the same way. Before levering a rock into place dig a depression where it is to sit, then bury at least a third of the rock so it seems to be thrust up from the earth rather than resting on top of it.

Keep in mind the occurrence of rocks in nature. Use rocks as natural outcroppings. Use large mountain rock, when you can, not field boulders. Always try to get mossy rocks rather than those from a quarry.

Rocks must be firmly placed and must look permanent—never standing on end or heaped into a meaningless jumble. Don't attempt to create solitary cliffs or mountains in miniature. Instead, try to reproduce full-scale sections of a natural scene.

If a rock has a flat top, the top should be fairly level rather than tipped far out of the horizontal.

If you have a rock that is such a shape that you can't set it deeply into the ground without making it look altogether lost, you can prop it up on the surface by using small stones underneath.

Once it's stabilized, pack soil between the small stones, then all around them to build up the earth to the base of the larger rock. Once moss or a ground cover has been established the large rock will appear to be set solidly in the earth.

The test of good rock work is its appearance before planting. It should be beautiful and complete in its own design without planting. If you have to use plants to cover a great many mistakes in rock placement, you will not have a good framework.

If you are using gravel or sand along with larger rocks, locate the big rocks first then fill in the rest of the area with the small stuff. You'll have an easier time and everything will fit together better.

How to Use Gravel

Cobbles are large-sized gravel, anywhere from 2 inches to 6 inches in diameter. Usually they are smooth and rounded.

You can use cobbles to form a stream bed—either to carry water or to create a dry stream—and to suggest a beach. Cobbles can be set into

CAST CONCRETE makes a foundation for support post at left, is blended with natural stone by gravel. In small garden at right, natural stone texture matches texture of the lantern.

ZEN DRY GARDEN is test of designer's ingenuity to make subtle understatement. A few rocks and some simple plantings create scene. The two upright rocks suggest mountains with waterfall.

concrete to form a pond bottom. They make a handsome looking path but unfortunately not one you can walk on with any comfort unless the rocks are set fairly close together in a bed of mortar with a flat surface up.

Instead of using the usual rain trough and downspout to carry away eave drip, you might employ an old Japanese trick. Find the exact line of the eave drip on the ground. Dig a trench along this line, about 6 inches deep and 6 to 10 inches wide, sloping the trench down at one end for drainage. Line the trench with concrete and when it sets fill the ditch with 3-inch cobbles, either leaving a slight depression in the center or making the rocks flush across the top. If you wish, you can edge the trench with a line of larger rocks.

The stones will keep the eave drip from fur-
rowing the ground and prevent mud from splashing, and the trench will carry off the water. It's a pleasant sight, especially when it's raining.

Use gravel to make mounds and depressions around larger rocks, much in the same way you'd shape soil. Though this is not a true dry garden it can form a small space garden or be part of a larger garden.

Loose gravel or small cobbles should be confined by header boards or other solid material, such as rocks or an edging made with vertical stakes or saplings. Edging boards can be concealed by letting a ground cover grow out and over them.

The ground under graveled areas should be smooth and tamped. Curve or slope paths or low areas so water will drain off.

IMPORTANT FUNCTION of garden elements is unifying house and surroundings. This is illustrated by fence and path, leading from house out into garden, small fence with stepping stones around it.

. . . GRAVEL

Larger-sized gravels are used to form the "sea" in a classical water basin arrangement (see page 136). A gravel mulch 2 or 3 inches deep around tree bases or around larger stones of a path is pleasant to look at.

To figure out how much gravel you'll need for an area, pace off the perimeter to estimate the square feet to be covered, then decide how deep the gravel should be. For a path, 1 inch is a good average depth—if you use much more than that, you'll have trouble walking in it; any less will be kicked around.

Don't try to haul large loads of gravel, even in a sturdy wheelbarrow. The wheelbarrow may hold up but your back won't. About 12 shovelfuls in a small wheelbarrow is a comfortable weight to load, wheel, and empty. If you buy small amounts of gravel in sacks, don't try to spread it directly from the sack. It's a lot easier to transport the sack in a wheelbarrow or hand truck and shovel the contents onto the ground.

Start dumping the gravel at the farthest point from the pile. Then you won't have to push the loaded wheelbarrow through the gravel.

Use the back of a metal rake to spread piles of gravel you move in. Spread each pile as you bring it in so you know about where to dump the next one.

Have a small stockpile of extra gravel on hand to fill in thin spots.

How Gravel is Sold

You can buy crushed rock or natural gravel. Crushed rock is made from larger rocks. It has sharp edges and points and packs more tightly than natural gravel. Natural gravel is rounded by the action of glaciers, streams, and the sea.

In the grading process, gravel is washed over screens with apertures of various sizes. Gravel is commonly available in the following sizes (diameter in inches): $1/4$, $3/8$, $5/8$, $7/8$, $1 1/2$, and $2 1/4$.

One cubic yard of gravel covers about 150 square feet to a depth of 2 inches. A minimum truckload is often 5 cubic yards (the price per yard is higher if you order less than a truckload). Most sand and gravel companies also sell 100-

pound sacks of various kinds of gravel, and many garden supply yards have fill-it-yourself bins where you can buy gravel by the sack.

Constructing a Zen Type of Garden

Usually the flat Zen garden is made to suggest a seascape, with raked sand or gravel serving as water and a few rocks serving as islands. True sand is usually too fine, since it tends to blow around in a strong wind and wash away in a heavy rain. Gravel of 1/4-inch mesh is about the best; it is large enough to stay in place, yet small enough to hold a raked design.

You'll do better using an off-white colored gravel (but avoid such wild types as red rock or green gravels). Stark white is unnatural and can be glaring in the summer sun. Light gray gravel looks good when combined with darker, almost black rocks.

If you plan a flat sand garden outside, prepare the area by clearing the ground of all weeds and rocks. Tamp or roll the earth until it's smooth and compact. If you don't expect to use any plants in the area, treat the ground with weed killer or spread polyethylene sheeting or builder's paper over the space the garden will occupy.

After locating the stone groupings and setting the rocks, spread out the gravel to a depth of about 3 inches, leveling it with a rake.

To create a design in the gravel, you can use a level-head garden rake (not a grass rake), or you can make your own special sand rake by cutting a saw-tooth edge in a 1-foot length of 1 x 4 lumber. Drill a hole in the board so you can fit in a long wooden dowel for a handle.

In raking a design, begin with the "island" rocks, or any rocks that project into the edges of the gravel, rake a circular pattern around them, raking a circular series of lines around them the width of the rake head. The idea is to create what looks like a series of ripples around the rocks, much like the circular ripples that spread out from a pebble thrown into a pond.

If there are any bridge supports or deck piers in the gravel, rake a circular pattern around them.

Next, rake the open area by drawing the rake generally parallel to the edges of the garden. When these lines begin to approach the circular lines blend the two together.

 Garden Planning Checklist

■ Draw a master plan of the area as it is now, indicating roughly the location of existing plants. By using ruled graph paper you can establish a fairly accurate scale. Be sure to include structures such as the house, fences, or paved areas.

■ Using sheets of thin tissue paper over the master plan, sketch your design ideas, showing walks, stone groupings, points of interest.

■ When you arrive at a plan that looks good (it may take many tissues) you might make a simple table-top model in three dimensions. Use earth, sand, pebbles, and wads of green paper to give you a better idea of how various elements will work together.

■ Outside, lay a "newspaper pattern" using flat sheets of newspaper for path stones and crumpling up several sheets for larger rocks. Poke stakes (3 to 5 feet long) into the ground for trees and shrubs. Start by working from your sketches and tray landscape, then move things around for a final arrangement.

■ When you're comfortable with the basic arrangement and feel you're ready to commit your plan, order materials. Have the most unwieldy materials unloaded as close as possible to where you plan to use them to save you extra labor.

■ In actually constructing the garden there are six steps you should follow to be able to allow for further changes if the need arises. First, install any underground lines the garden may require: water, drainage, electricity.

■ Next, build such major structures as fences, tea houses, or arbors.

■ Then, do the earth work: construct pools, dig out stream beds, move soil for mounds, scoop out low areas, level or slope bases for paths and steps.

■ Move rocks and stones into place (details on large rocks are given in the chapter on stone).

■ Locate and put in your plant materials starting with trees, then shrubs, then ground covers. You have one last chance to try a final arrangement or two. Before digging planting holes set the plant containers (or balled trees) where they are to go and look at them from all sides. If one doesn't look just right where it is, try it somewhere else, working around your earth-rock framework.

■ Finally, add accessories, such as lanterns, basins, pagodas, wells, bridges, bonsai.

If the garden has a straight edge, you might rake parallel to it but in a gentle wavy pattern to create the effect of waves washing up against a beach.

Usually a single pass with the rake for each series of lines is enough. Don't work the rake back and forth, but pull it smoothly, letting its own weight form the impression. Avoid making cross-hatch patterns or complex designs in the gravel. The more simple the design, the better.

There is a flat, raked-sand garden within the Japanese Tea Garden in San Francisco's Golden Gate Park.

SPECIAL-PURPOSE STONES

Stone makes one of the best transitions between house and garden. Most family gardens in Japan use a large, flat stone between the veranda and ground level. It serves as a step as well as a shoe stone—the Japanese remove their shoes before entering a house. It also forms a natural connection between the house and the garden.

A shoe stone should be a sizeable natural rock with a flat top (at least 1 x 2 feet at the top), or you can use one or more pieces of cut stone, such as old granite curbing. If the shoe stone is more than a foot in height, use a second-level or third-level stone to form steps.

Stones can be put to other utilitarian purposes. You can use them to form a base for a lantern or a bonsai. You can make a bench or resting place. In the tea garden, you use special stones to hold a water bucket or a tea kettle.

For a Center of Interest, Think Big

You can sometimes achieve a very special effect by landscaping a small garden entirely around a large boulder. A 2500 or 3000-pound rock sounds formidable but makes an impressive point of interest in the garden.

If you can acquire a large rock that has depressions or holes in it, plant ferns or dwarf conifers and encourage the growth of moss.

The boulder that resembles a large outcropping can have a sculptural beauty worth dramatizing as the most important feature in the garden. Such a rock even has special climates around it. There are cool sides where you can grow shade-loving plants, and hot sides for plants that take full sun. Many ferns and azaleas will do well in the shade; mugho pine, some of the junipers, and low-growing cotoneaster will take to the sunny side.

Sometimes you can use a sledge hammer and wedge on a fair-sized boulder to split it along seams (do this in the place where the rock will stay rather than trying to transport the parts afterward). Separate the sections a few inches, then fill in between them with a loamy soil mixture, blending in sand or peat moss to ensure good drainage. Plant ground cover or cultivate moss; put in shrublets, alpine plants, ferns, or low-growing perennials. Continue some of the planting in the soil around the rock to blend it with its surroundings. This arrangement is essentially a scree, a bed of fragmented rock. The more porous the growing medium is, the better the growth of scree plants. The one essential is plenty of water.

Often, a large boulder plus a few plants will convey the natural feeling the Japanese garden strives to capture without your having to add accessories such as lanterns and walks.

The Japanese like to name things—if not for spiritual reasons, then for shape or association. Even function is touched by the poetic to give such designations as the thinking stone (a place where one may sit and enjoy the surroundings), the gull-resting stone (whose association is obvious), the easy resting stone (a seat for the master of the house).

For a Small Area, Think Small

There are several ways of creating a small, intimate garden for an area with limited space without compressing an entire Japanese garden. Any of the corners of gardens shown in this book could serve as a garden in itself. Though creating some of them may strain the dictum repeated in these pages that a Japanese garden should contain stone, plants, and water, their feeling is unmistakably Japanese. For example:

■ Use a stunted tree with an interesting form (or a bonsai) by itself or in the company of a couple of rocks, arranging the parts in an irregular triangular configuration.
■ Make a rock grouping with three or five unequal-sized rocks. Use the rocks alone, or add a small plant.
■ Arrange a stone lantern, a rock or two, and a few simple plants in such a way that each complements the other.
■ Make a *tsukubai* water basin grouping (see

TWO LARGE STONES form center of interest in back corner of garden. Junipers in front of rocks soften visual mass. Note how bamboo stems repeat lines of fence in background. (Design, George Kubota.)

IMPRESSIVE WATERFALL drops in a series of cascades for a vertical distance of almost 20 feet. The water appears and disappears, finally splashes noisily into a pond.

page 136) using a stone basin, rocks, and plants. Locate it either near a fence, or in an outer corner of the garden.

■ Create a *chozubachi* water basin grouping (see page 137) near the house using a basin, stones, and a simple open fence.

Using Stones Around Water

In the city of Okayama, Japan, there is a large garden that was built in the late 1600's. A huge boulder forms a steep bank of a pond. The boulder has many cracks and looks as if it had been fitted together like a gigantic, three-dimensional jigsaw puzzle.

This is exactly what happened. When the garden was being built the stone was found many miles away on one of the islands in the inland sea. It was the perfect stone for the location at the end of the pond—no other would do. Since it was too large to be moved, the stone was carefully broken into almost a hundred pieces, moved to the garden, then reassembled.

This is a good example of how the Japanese try to keep natural elements in their true settings. The stone occurred in a natural water setting, and it was used in a man-made water setting.

The Westerner need not go to such lengths as using only water-associated stones around the water in his own garden but he should avoid using stones that look out of place and are incongruous in certain situations.

The "best" stones to use around water are those that have a smooth surface that actually appears water-worn. Quarried stone, which has broken surfaces and sharp edges, usually is too

MODEST CATARACT in private garden issues out of rock grouping as if from hidden spring, twists and turns for about 5 feet among rocks and baby's tears. (Design, George Kubota.)

mechanical looking to be used in association with water. Volcanic rock is too ragged and too dry looking.

The rocks you use around water should themselves have a flowing, smooth and peaceful appearance. This is especially important if you are only suggesting water, as in a dry stream.

Use stone to make the transition between water and land. Locate several good-sized rocks to sit half in the water, half on the land, to blend the two. Use a large, flat rock to create a promontory on which you might set a lantern. (The lantern-on-a-rock-jutting-into-water is a classical scheme that serves two poetical purposes. By day the arrangement is reflected prettily in the water and at night the lantern guides boaters to a nearby landing.)

A flat stone is often located at the bottom of a waterfall to break up the falling water. A rock with a flat top is often made to overhang a stream, thus symbolically providing a seat for fishing or for viewing the water. Sometimes a large flat stone is placed in shallow water so the shadows of goldfish swimming over it can be seen and enjoyed.

Moving water with few ripples and little air is less alive than foamy, white water. Place a stone in a stream in such a way that the water will be diverted around it and create eddies and splashes. It not only looks good, it sounds good.

Stones for a Waterfall

The classical waterfall arrangement is made around selected rock forms, each of which has a specific function and a special name. Although

THREE WAYS TO MOVE heavy object without strain: Slide, using a shovel, piece of canvas, or board. Lift, using tripod and pulley system. Roll, using steel bar or plank as a lever.

. . . WATERFALL STONES

it isn't necessary to follow the classical version precisely, the basic scheme makes good sense and can provide a model for any waterfall.

Page 88 gives some practical suggestions on constructing a waterfall based in part on the following ways certain rocks are used.

There are five types of stones used with waterfalls: the largest rocks are two flanking stones, located to either side of the cascade and slightly forward of it. They give emphasis to the water by visually containing it laterally. The bases of the flanking stones should sit well into the earth and their tops should extend 6 inches to 1 foot above the edge of the cascade, depending on the size of the falls. The flanking stones may be upright or can lean slightly into the cascade.

The stone over which the water falls is called the mirror stone. It may be a large single rock or may be made up of several smaller stones. It should sit snugly and securely between the flanking stones, touching them. A mirror stone with a level lip that overhangs the rest of the rock will produce a cascade that drops straight down in a wide sheet. One with an irregular or grooved lip will produce a cataract that bounces and splashes in its drop. The latter type of cascade has a more informal feeling about it.

The mirror stone should sit well back, or the flanking stones well forward. This gives the falls dimension, frames the cascade, and gives mass to the flanking stones. If the mirror stone leans forward, the falls will tend to shoot out away from it; if it leans back slightly, the water will follow the line of its face.

A smaller stone is often used at the foot of each flanking stone. These base stones help to stabilize the mass of the flankers and provide a transition between their vertical lines and the horizontal plane of the water at their foot. Base stones should be located for the most part in the pool created by the falls, several inches in front of the flanking stones. The base stones should be about one-fourth the height of the flankers.

A dividing stone is often used above the mirror stone and a little way back. It should be in the small pond where the falls originates and should lean back slightly to give the water greater action as it starts over the falls. It should be smaller than the base stones.

Another water dividing stone (or several smaller stones) is usually used in the fall basin to break up the water and create a cataract as it starts down the stream. The lower dividing stone should lean toward the falls and should be located at the center of the basin, a little to the rear of the base stones.

Often a sizeable vertical rock placed at the base of a waterfall helps to create a greater feeling of depth. Such a rock should be about a third the height of the falls and sit to one side of the cascade, behind the lower water dividing stone.

HOW TO HANDLE STONE

Without some kind of tool you shouldn't attempt to move or lift a stone weighing more than about 50 pounds. It's not just the lifting but the accompanying twisting, pushing, and pulling to jockey a rock into place that can give you Monday morning back. If you have a lot of small rocks to move, use all of the mechanical help you can get. Don't be in a hurry to get all of the stones shifted and settled at one time—there's always another weekend.

Never try to move a large rock downhill by yourself. You may get it going all right but controlling it or stopping it is another matter. With bars, two men can roll a good-sized rock, if it isn't too squarish.

A builder's wheelbarrow is handy for moving stones up to 300 pounds in size. Turn the wheelbarrow on its side, roll the stone into it, then get someone to help you right the wheelbarrow. A hand truck is useful for moving stones, but you'll probably have to rope the big ones on to keep them in place while you trundle them around.

A block and tackle rig is slow but effective for moving large rocks, if you have a large tree handy for anchoring the block. Tie a thick padding of gunny sacks around the tree trunk to protect it from the abrasion of the rope.

On flat ground use the age-old method of moving large objects on rollers. Get the rock onto a piece of plywood (1/2-inch thick), which in turn rests on three or four parallel rollers—round wooden stakes or 3-inch pipe. Push the rock and board together until they've moved off one of the rollers, which you then pick up and move from the back to the front. You'll have to go pretty much in a straight line, but you can move a good-sized rock this way.

To hoist a large rock, rig a pulley system from a tripod made with 2 x 4's. Or, you can rent a chain hoist.

With patience and just a little muscle you and a helper can move a 500-pound rock using a steel bar or a stout piece of lumber as levers. A wooden lever won't scratch or chip the surface of the stone; if you use a bar, pad it to protect the stone.

STREET-SIDE LANDSCAPING is simple, yet makes definite statement with Oriental overtones. Pebbles extend from curb to redwood pilings; smaller gravel covers mound. (Design, George Kubota.)

A PROFUSION of plants, but good areas of open space plus careful pruning keep garden in proper scale. This garden "borrows" trees and masses of greenery from distant properties. (Design, F. H. Mick.)

The Right Way to Use Plants

The Oriental look...using trees, shrubs, flowers ... the ever-useful bamboos ... ground covers...plants around water

The Japanese have a way with plants. Their country is one of great natural beauty, but time and population growth have worn away much of the natural landscape. Over many centuries the Japanese have mastered the art of bringing the feeling of nature into the garden through the use of stone, water . . . and plants.

It's not only the presence of plants that help give a garden a natural look. It's also the way that you use them. Following are some general guides to follow in your planting if you want to capture a natural feeling.

■ Build the secondary garden framework (stones come first) with evergreen plants. Start with trees. They're the most stable and permanent in feeling and they establish reference points.

■ Give plants space. Don't locate them individually at random all over the garden, but also don't bunch up everything until it's a solid mass. Group together several plants related in form or texture but different in height. Vertical space can be as important as horizontal.

■ Limit the variety of your plantings. The Japanese may plant an entire garden with azaleas, bamboo, and a pine; or only one kind of plant; or, simplest of all, only a single specimen plant— a beautifully curved pine or a gnarled old plum tree—set off against a rock in a carpet of gravel or on a floor of clean earth. After a certain point, the more variety you create in the garden, the less unity it will have.

■ Don't locate all of your plants on the same level. Even in a small garden create raised or sunken areas or make mounds with low-growing plants themselves. Differences in level help to prevent monotony and give dimension.

■ To make a small garden seem larger, leave the central area clear of trees and shrubs and use them along the sides or in corners. Keep the middle open or make a simple arrangement of three rocks.

■ Use flowering plants sparingly. If you want cut flowers, grow them in a separate area. If you do use a limited number of flowers in the main garden, locate them between evergreens; it shows them off better when they are in bloom and helps to subdue them when they are bare of blossoms. Keep in mind that too many colors in the Japanese garden break up its unity.

■ Combine plants and other natural materials

according to their associations in nature. Don't mix the plants of forest, seaside, and mountain.

■ Enjoy such flowering shrubs as azaleas primarily for their permanent structure, not just for their flowers.

■ Keep plants in proper proportion by pruning them regularly. Overgrown plants lose their personality and crowd a garden. (However, don't shape plants into unnatural forms.)

■ Don't overlook the beauty of winter form in deciduous trees and shrubs.

■ Look at fall-colored leaves and spring buds of trees such as maples and sumacs the same way you look at flowers.

■ Don't have all close-up scenes in the garden. To give depth to even a small area, create distant views (even if they are only a few feet away against a fence) with a grove of bamboo, a dwarf tree, or a small rock grouping.

THE ORIENTAL LOOK

What is the Oriental look in plants? Is it restricted to the traditional plants of the Far East? To give your garden the Oriental look, must you use only plants native to the Orient?

Quite the contrary. All around us are native and introduced plants with that special quality that comes to mind when you speak of an Oriental garden. That special quality most often is an understatement. Generally, it's the opposite effect from that of a full-blown flowering individual which saturates the eye with color. It's beauty that increases with a second look. It's wrapped up in branch structure, leaf pattern, shadow movement—subtle restrained effects for quiet appreciation.

Learn to see those characteristics in plants. Look at plants as more than something green in

MOOD IS SET BY PLANTS coordinated with stone. Left: black pine and creeping fig frame door (Design, Andre Cuenoud). Right: young trees blend with fence, background (Design, George Kubota).

OLD, ESTABLISHED Japanese garden is a wealth of evergreens, some full height, others trained to stay a few feet tall. Tall trees in far background aren't part of garden but are visually borrowed.

the garden. Look at them with an eye to dramatic forms (but learn to avoid odd and distracting forms). Utilize textures—the smooth surface of magnolia leaves, the coarse bark of pines. Take advantage of striking foliage patterns—the regular arrangement of an aralia's leaves, the rich disarray of heavenly bamboo.

Basic Plants for the Japanese Garden

Almost any plant material can be used in the Japanese garden if it's used in the right way. Since the aim of a Japanese garden is to imitate nature by using natural materials, there is really no restriction on what plants might be used to achieve that end. Following is a summary of plants that are typically found in the Japanese garden and are Oriental in feeling.

■ *Deciduous Trees.* Birch, buckeye or horse-chestnut, ginkgo, Japanese maples (many varieties), larch, oak, persimmon, pomegranate, sweet olive, willow, zelkova.

■ *Evergreen Trees.* Ash, cedar, cypress, fig, fir, hemlock, holly, Japanese yew, juniper, loquat, magnolia (evergreen or deciduous tree or shrub), pine.

■ *Flowering Trees.* Buckeye or horsechestnut, coral tree, crape myrtle, dogwood, empress tree, flowering almond, flowering cherry, flowering peach, flowering plum, goldenchain tree, magnolia, orchid tree.

■ *Shrubs.* Abelia, aralia, aucuba, azalea. bamboo (really grasses), barberry, bayberry, daphne, dogwood (shrub or tree), elaegnus, euonymus, fatsia, heavenly bamboo, holly, Japanese privet, pieris, rhododendron, podocarpus, privet (shrub or tree), service berry (shrub or tree).

■ *Flowers.* Anemone, camellia, chrysanthemum, crocus, gentian, hydrangea, iris, jonquil, peony.

■ *Vines.* Akebia, bittersweet, clematis, honeysuckle, jasmine, wisteria.

APPEALING ENTRY from street is created with bold gate and wall, whose lines are softened with plantings of wisteria, juniper, spruce. Note shrubs over lower wall behind juniper. (Design, F. H. Mick.)

■ *Grasses and Ground Covers.* Baby's tears, bamboo (dwarf varieties), carpet bugle, Irish moss, mondo grass, Scotch moss, Spanish moss, wild strawberry.

■ *Trees and Shrubs for Autumn Color.* Ash, beech, Chinese flame tree, Chinese pistache, cotoneaster, dogwood, *Fothergilla*, ginkgo, hawthorn, Japanese barberry, Japanese cryptomeria, Katsura, maple, persimmon, redbud, service berry, smoke tree, sumac, sour gum.

Planting That Problem Corner

In a city garden, a narrow walkway, or an out-of-the-way corner of the back yard, plants often have four strikes against them in the way of limited space, too little or too much sun, bad air, and poor soil. Since such an area is relatively confined, most trees are out of the question, even if they could manage to survive.

These challenging spots are a "natural" for a small Japanese style garden. For instance, you can design a garden around rocks, using some interesting stones, pebbles, and sand. Limit the plantings to only the most rugged and hardy. Following are some choices for such problem corners:

■ *Trees and Shrubs.* Carissa, cotoneaster, firethorn, holly, Japanese black pine, junipers, lily-of the-valley shrub, yew.

■ *Ground Covers.* Ivy, Japanese spurge, periwinkle, rockcress.

■ *Miscellaneous Plants.* Blue fescue (clumping ornamental grass), oxalis (blooming perennial), yarrow (blooming perennial).

TREES AS DESIGN ELEMENTS

Whether you are starting a garden from scratch, or modifying what you already have to give the place a Japanese feeling, trees are important design elements.

 **How to Choose a Tree**

Several commonly available trees that can be used in Japanese gardens are illustrated below. These by no means represent the only trees that are appropriate but are intended as a guide to general form and application.

PINE TREES FOR GARDEN STRUCTURE

ITALIAN STONE PINE *JEFFREY PINE* *LODGEPOLE PINE* *ALEPPO PINE*

TREES FOR COLOR ACCENT

GOLDENRAIN TREE *FLOWERING CHERRY* *HAWTHORN* *RED HORSECHESTNUT*

TREES WITH DRAMATIC FORMS

GINKGO *SILK TREE* *REDBUD* *WHITE BIRCH*

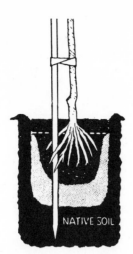

BARE ROOT planting requires 1:3 mix (organic material: native soil—light area), plus 1:1 mix (dark area). See details, page 54.

BALLED AND BURLAPPED trees and shrubs should go into planting hole twice size of plant's root system. See page 53.

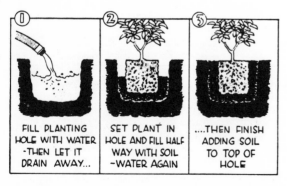

FILL PLANTING HOLE WITH WATER -THEN LET IT DRAIN AWAY...

SET PLANT IN HOLE AND FILL HALF WAY WITH SOIL -WATER AGAIN

....THEN FINISH ADDING SOIL TO TOP OF HOLE

CONTAINER-GROWN plants need to have roots loosened at bottom, sides of ball after being removed from can. See page 53.

. . . TREES

With a brand new garden, set trees in place before any other plants. With an already established garden, the existing trees often indicate how far in the Japanese direction you can go; they will also be guides for the type and size of the rest of the plantings you wish to add.

Here's an obvious but good example of how a certain kind of existing tree might entirely inhibit your plans for a Japanese garden. If the garden area were a portion of a former date orchard, well-planted with palms, you'd probably have a difficult time designing a Japanese garden around such trees. The palm just doesn't have an Oriental character about it.

On the other hand, if you have some old apricot or plum trees on your property, they can provide a very good basic structure around which to plan an Oriental garden.

Fortunately, there are not too many trees that —once you have them—foil the possibilities of a Japanese style of landscaping.

In Planning Trees, Think Ahead

Before heading for the nursery to buy those three deodar cedars, because they happen to be on sale and because they grow fast, consider the deodar and how it grows. You may indeed need a fast-grower but do you have room for a tree that reaches 80 feet in height and half that in width? You may be charmed by the foliage and blossoms of a Japanese plum and you may think of the fruit as a bonus. But also think of when the fruit starts ripening and begins attracting birds and flies. In any landscaping situation—but most especially in the Japanese garden—putting in a new tree is a step that requires careful thought.

Aside from their esthetic qualities, there are two important factors to keep in mind when planning and choosing trees: their ultimate height, and how fast they reach it. The really fast growers should be selected with caution. You may find that you can't easily train a 50-foot tree to a modest 20 feet. Also, a fast grower can quickly take over a small property. Shallow, invasive root systems or easily broken branches (common with some really fast ones, such as eucalyptus) can cause trouble. Gardening under trees that drop many leaves can be difficult.

Plan for trees that seem to you to work best in your specific situation but reserve the final choice until after you've talked with a local nurseryman.

Don't place deciduous trees at the front of the garden where their bare winter branches may look cheerless and barren. Instead, put them against a fence, wall, or gate, where bare branches will cast interesting shadows. Exceptions are flowering fruit trees, which you may want to use as a seasonal center of interest.

If you can situate a flowering tree where it's visible from the house, as well as from the garden, you've gained another bonus. It's a Japanese tradition to plant a flowering plum or almond outside a guest room so it can be viewed from inside.

Use different forms or colors together for contrast and emphasis. The warm brilliance of Chinese pistache will be intensified if displayed against a background of darker evergreens. Don't carry the idea too far or its effect will be lost.

In planting a "forest" of trees, don't locate them in soldierly rows. Instead, bunch them in irregular groups of, say, two, three, and five trees ... much the same way groves occur in the wild.

Doing the Groundwork

It goes without saying that new plants should go into well prepared soil. If you start with good soil, your plants will look good; if you neglect the soil, your plants will reflect it.

If subsoil is hard packed, break it up by covering it with six inches of some sort of organic matter such as sawdust, peat moss, ground bark, or leaf mold—and churning it by rotary tilling.

In planting trees or shrubs follow good gardening practice, as described in the *Sunset Western Garden Book:* Dig the planting hole large enough to accommodate roots; for heavy soil, mix organic matter into the back-fill soil; adjust the depth so the old soil line at the base of the trunk is at grade level; work soil around all the roots; stake trees or tall shrubs.

If you buy plants in containers, have the nursery man cut the cans for you unless you expect to let them sit for several days before planting (or have the cans cut but then tie them together until you plant to keep roots from drying out).

Balled and burlapped shrubs and trees are sometimes easier to handle than those in cans. Burlap and twine are all that hold the root ball together, so handle with care. The burlap should be taut and tied securely, with no part of the root ball exposed. When bringing plants home make sure they won't roll around, and don't use the trunk as a handle (this applies to trees in cans as well); if the ball isn't tight, it will loosen even more. Be careful not to hit the ball against something while you're carrying it.

The planting hole for a balled or container-grown plant should be about twice as wide and one and a half times as deep as the root ball. Set the plant on a cushion of loose soil mix so the top of the root ball is slightly higher than the surrounding ground. Most plants have a best side that fits better with the surroundings. Before you

 Ways to Use Color in the Garden

Color plays a secondary role in the Japanese garden where evergreen trees and shrubs are used for a framework. Color is used very selectively for a center of interest, for special emphasis. Within the main garden it is seldom used in large mass. Here are some suggestions on how to use color in the Japanese garden.

■ *What Colors to Use.* Generally, the more brilliant the color, the more sparingly it should be used. Avoid bright yellows, reds, and blues in favor of the more earthy colors of deep orange (chrysanthemum), dark yellow, copper, and purple (as in autumn leaves).

■ *Where to Locate Color.* As much as possible limit color to just a few places in the garden—it'll have more meaning than if it's scattered everywhere. Back it up with a darker background, such as a fence or wall or mass of evergreen planting. Azaleas and rhododendrons look good massed on a hillside or mound.
■ *How to Use Color.* As well as limiting the locations for color, limit varieties both of colors and plants. This will help unify the plantings. Make strong use of the many variations of green in the conifers. Take advantage of seasonal changes in trees by using the colors of autumn leaves, spring blossoms, and bare winter branches.

fill in the hole, rotate the plant until it faces in the right direction.

Fill the hole about halfway with soil mixed with organic matter, firming it with a stick. If a supporting stake is needed, put it in now rather than driving it in later so you don't damage the roots. If it's a balled and burlapped plant, loosen the twine and burlap at the top now. Fill the hole to the top with soil. Build a water basin by hoeing up a circle of soil. Soak well, filling the basin two or three times.

Bare-root trees, shrubs, and vines are available during winter and early spring. Nurseries offer a wide selection of deciduous plants and you pay less for them than if you wait to buy the same plants in containers months later.

Bare-root plants are easy to handle, since there is no root ball to contend with. Dig a planting hole twice the size of the plant's root system, drive in the supporting stake, and form a mound of soil in the bottom of the hole. Trim off any broken roots, spread the roots over the planting mound, and fill the hole with soil or mix, working it carefully around the roots. Build up a circle of soil around the hole and fill the basin several times with water.

There is no rule that says a tree must be planted in a vertical position. In nature trees are just as likely to be leaning, and training a young tree in your garden to grow in this fashion does a great deal to help you break away from a formal, strait-laced approach.

Keep Your Trees Looking Good

If there is any secret to making a garden look Oriental, it surely has its roots in pruning techniques, and the key word in Japanese pruning methods is control. Once the skeleton of main trunk and supporting branches is established, the basic form is maintained so the tree never grows beyond garden scale. This technique emphasizes a tree's horizontal branching pattern and is aimed at preventing vertical growth from obscuring the structure.

All ornamental trees require careful training the first few years in the garden, but after about the fourth year most require little further care except to control size and shape. Developing the open Japanese effect in a mature tree that has received standard pruning takes three to five years, but you'll see a definite change the first season if you remove all dead, weak, and crossing branches, then thin the remaining branches to form a pleasing pattern.

In addition to training the branches and trunk of a tree to establish a form, you should also thin out the foliage to create masses that will contrast with open spaces and with the bare trunk.

Some Japanese gardeners shape certain trees—usually evergreens—by clipping twigs and leaves back to form disc-like shapes. This treatment is usually considered too formal and out of keeping with a natural feeling. Another method is to cut back all vertical branchlets at several levels in order that branches will have a definite flattish form. This can be very effective as long as the foliage groups are asymmetrical around the tree and do not form a regular series of rings.

Supple branches of trees and shrubs can be trained by tying on weights (stones or large fishing sinkers) to pull them down and form a graceful arch. Use enough weight to bring the branch down to where you want it, but not so much that it will be in danger of breaking.

Don't be afraid to cut out excess branches of a tree or dense shrub. Learn to recognize the personality of each plant and emphasize that personality or character by pruning and shaping.

You may like to see branches in flat tiers with considerable space between. You may prefer a spiral pattern, or a pronounced irregularity with masses of comparatively thick growth balanced by open areas. Whatever your choice is, don't allow your enthusiasm to create freak forms alien to natural growth.

Carefully controlled pruning tends to dwarf a plant and permits control over the size to which it will grow. Natural dwarfs, such as mugho pine, are a pleasure to train and control, but trying to keep up with a forest giant such as a redwood can be a never-ending job.

Low-sweeping branches are a favorite in the Japanese garden. By severe initial pruning on selected branches, cut back all vertical growth. Weight a branch or pull it down gently and gradually over many months by using wire attached to stakes driven into the ground. Keep top growth pinched back to emphasize a spreading horizontal form. Eventually, when the branch has grown enough that it doesn't require weights or wires to keep it down, you can construct a trellis under it for support. Train such branches to lean out over water or to cross in front of a stone lantern.

CENTER OF INTEREST is handsome pine with twisted trunk made visible by heavy pruning, careful training. Gate, maple, and low hedge in foreground all frame tree. Light color of foliage is due to bright sun.

THE VALUE OF SHRUBS

Shrubs provide screening; they soften architectural lines; they help provide a transition from house to garden; they provide contrasts in color, mass, and texture.

The best shrubs for permanent landscaping are those which grow slowly but once established maintain their character year after year. Unless fast growers are kept in hand by pruning, they may overpower a garden by hiding rocks and spreading out to take too much space.

Never judge a shrub strictly by its flowers, or even its lack of them. Look for form and foliage.

In the Japanese garden, avoid every possible temptation to train shrubs or trees in topiary fashion. If a plant suggests, to your eye, a pagoda or some animal form, do all in your power to modify its shape. Not too many years ago it was thought that a garden full of shrubs trimmed in the shape of gamboling lambs or quaint lanterns was in the Oriental spirit.

It isn't.

Following are some typically Japanese evergreen shrubs and one grass used as a shrub, along with some hints on their use and care.

■ *Japanese Aucuba.* Polished, dark green leaves; some varieties have variegated leaves blotched with white or yellow. Use in deep shade, around streams or ponds. Give ample water. Once planted, don't dig around roots. May eventually grow to 10 feet, but mild pruning will control it. Dwarf varieties are also available.

■ *Azaleas and Rhododendrons.* Thousands of species and varieties, some of which prefer shade, others full sun. Some are evergreen, some deciduous. All require a constant moisture supply and soil that drains rapidly. Plant in groups of all the same color flowers. Always remove the spent flowers, to assure good blooms the following season. Prune to maintain desired form immediately after the last flowers fade.

■ *Heavenly Bamboo.* A handsome, delicate looking shrub that requires little care. The Japanese often plant heavenly bamboo just outside a door

SHRUBS, ROCKS, old millstone steps combine to blend intimate garden with home in Hawaii. Nandina at right, ervatamia at left, sedum (ground cover), leopard plant, eugenia. (Design, Takano Nakamura.)

TREES TRAINED AS SHRUBS have distinctive personality for center of interest. In either picture, cover rock with hand and see how it is essential to entire composition, helping to stabilize plant.

leading to the garden, where, as legend has it, they can tell it of their bad dreams and thus prevent them from coming true. Leaves will turn fiery crimson in winter. Color is better if grown in full sun; in shade it is a soft, pale green.

■ *Podocarpus.* Small tree, or large shrub, depending on how you train it. The foliage is graceful and willowy or ferny. Use near the house or for close-up spots in the garden. Some varieties like sun; others prefer shade. Will grow to tree size, but slowly, so you can easily keep it under control. Good plant for an indoor garden.

■ *Bamboo.* Bamboo is perhaps the most Japanese of all plants and can be used almost anywhere in the garden. Though classed as a grass, it is often used as a shrub. There are two general types: clumping and running. The latter must be contained or it can take over a garden. Bamboo will grow in sun or shade but requires good drainage and plenty of water. To control, cut canes at or just below ground level. Most varieties are easy to divide. See details later in this chapter.

WHAT ABOUT FLOWERS?

Plantings in the traditional Japanese garden are chiefly green. There are several reasons for this. With the exception of deciduous plants, there are few changes over the year—foliage generally remains green, which is in keeping with the feeling of permanence and restfulness. Withered flower stems and faded blooms can give a garden an unkempt look. Rather than bold colors and exotic flower forms, the Japanese prefer the subtle, earthy hues of an autumn-tinted maple, or the gentle freshness of a flowering cherry tree blooming in the spring.

If you wish to use flowers in your garden, remember these suggestions to help retain the Oriental feeling:

■ Avoid large beds or long borders of flowers in the main garden.

■ Keep flower plantings unified by having a

COLOR WITHOUT FLOWERS *is provided by variegated Japanese acuba, whose leaves are splashed with white or gold. Low-growing bamboo blends fence line to ground, looks good with bamboo rail.*

... FLOWERS

group of one kind in a specific area, another kind in another area.

■ One type of flower per garden is best. Two or three are all right, depending on the size of the garden. More than three kinds are probably too many for even the largest garden.

■ Locate flower groups where they will enhance their immediate surroundings as well as the entire garden.

The flowers typically found in Japanese gardens are always used with restraint and with purpose. The following are representative, though by no means complete; some are annuals, some perennials, but most are shrubs.

Azaleas and rhododendrons (both shrubs) are often used in mass plantings—an entire hillside may be covered with evergreen azaleas for a solid

DELIGHTFUL PATH of stepping stones winds casually through garden. Trees and shrubs were carefully located to provide spots of interest to the stroller without entirely separating path from rest of garden.

area of color. Chrysanthemums—both annual and perennial—are planted in sunny places, often in between low shrubs so the blossoms stand out against a contrasting foliage; chrysanthemums give warm yellows, oranges, and browns in late summer and fall. Tree peony is a traditional favorite but should not be used to an excess, since the flowers can reach a very large size; use them against a fence. Japanese iris is frequently used around water or along dry streams; its swordlike leaves are appealing in their own right. *Daphne odora*, a low shrub, is prized for its delicate, spring fragrance and makes a handsome planting at the base of a large stone lantern. Camellia is a shrub grown as much for its dark, lustrous leaves as for its handsome flowers. Wisteria is trained on trellises or over arbors, where its twining woody trunk and long clusters of spring flowers help blend house and garden.

BAMBOO MEANS THE ORIENT

Few groups of plants suggest the Orient more effectively than the bamboos. Their sturdy stems and delicate foliage reflect a combination of strength and grace that has inspired generations of Oriental painters. Their sturdiness and quick

GROVE OF TIMBER BAMBOO stands out boldly against wooden fence. Leaves are complemented by foliage of accompanying ferns. Fallen bamboo leaves make good mulch. (Design, F. H. Mick.)

... PLANTING BAMBOO

growth make them excellent screens or bold vertical masses. And they are ideal container plants.

Bamboos are giant grasses with woody stems divided into sections. There are two types: running, and clumping. Running bamboos spread—and spread, and spread—unless their underground stems are confined. Clumping bamboos, as the name suggests, grow in clumps and spread more slowly.

Most kinds will grow in a pot, tub, or box, and most can adapt to being indoors for several months at a time as long as they are not kept in too warm a place. Container-grown bamboo should be watered and fed regularly.

Though they will grow in diffused light, bamboos prefer quite a bit of sun. Most will survive in poor soil, but they do best in loose, fairly rich soil. They need plenty of water, especially in the spring when new stems appear above ground.

You can plant bamboos from nursery containers at any time of the year. Dividing and transplanting bamboo already in the ground should be done from late fall to early spring.

Running bamboos should be contained unless you want the surrounding area totally covered. An 18-inch-deep barrier of sheet metal or pressed asbestos, or a poured concrete bulkhead, will confine most kinds, but some of the giant timber bamboos require barriers that go down to 3 feet. You can plant running bamboos in sunken lengths of flue tile, concrete pipe, or even oil drums with the bottoms removed.

When a planting of bamboo has grown out as

How to Use Bamboo in the Garden

Bamboo is used in the Japanese garden for the strong vertical lines of the stems and for the delicate grace of the foliage. Oriental gardeners have for centuries used bamboo for these same reasons as well as for its symbolism. It resists the storm but yields to it and rises again; it always remains green and youthful. The bamboo, the pine, and the winter-flowering plum—the three friends of winter—are symbols of strength, friendship, and dignified old age.

Bamboos are useful in the Western United States, in the deep South, and on the West Coast. In the northeastern and midwestern parts of the country you can't find many bamboos—or grow them well.

KINDS OF BAMBOO. Any of the bamboos will serve as screen plants. *Bambusa oldhami* will, in time, make a green curtain up to 60 feet high; Chinese goddess bamboo will make a filmy curtain of 6 feet or so. There are many intermediate sizes. With regular clipping, some of the smaller bamboos can be shaped into tight hedges anywhere from 2 to 20 feet tall.

You can also use bamboos much as you use more conventional shrubs and trees, either singly or in groups. The biggest clumping bamboos can supply overhead shade. The smaller clumping bamboos make fine background or filler shrubs and give good silhouettes against walls or fences.

Running bamboos can be used in the same way but you must limit their spread. Bamboos grouped with large-leafed plants—ginger or elephant ears—can create jungle effects in partially shaded areas.

The running types make very good ground covers.

Ground cover bamboos range from the 10-inch *Sasa pygmaea* to the 3-foot *S. humilis.*

WHERE TO USE BAMBOO. The Japanese like to see the strong vertical lines of the stem, arching patterns of the branches, and the delicate disposition of the leaves on the twig. They cultivate bamboo in this way to cast striking shadow patterns against a fence or on a deck.

One classical use of bamboo is in the entry garden, where stepping stones among carefully spaced tall timber bamboos are made to simulate a path through a grove.

Bamboo has a natural affinity for such textures as unfinished wood, adobe, stone, exposed aggregate, and gravel. Consequently it finds wide use in plantings near decks, engawa, paved areas, fences, patios, and dry landscapes.

DIVIDING AND PLANTING. To divide running types, uncover a thick underground stem and cut it about 12 inches from a main clump with a spade, axe, or saw. Dig the plant up with a good ball of soil and transplant. For the clumping type, tie at least four stems together to define the size of your division, dig down under that portion of the clump and separate it from the main plant with an ax or sharp spade.

Plant divisions in soil with good drainage and give them plenty of water. If you plant in full sun, shade the leaves for about a week.

You might have to stake a new plant for the first six months or so to prevent wind from toppling it before root growth anchors it. Use lengths of bamboo and they won't be discernible from the live stems.

VERSATILE BAMBOO can be used almost anywhere in the garden. At left, golden bamboo thrives in wet clay. Center, timber bamboo grows next to deck. Right, dwarf bamboo in poolside pocket.

far as you wish, keep it under control by breaking off the tender shoots as they appear. The Japanese study each shoot to determine whether it adds to the total effect and should therefore be allowed to develop, or whether another stem would be extraneous and should be removed. Large timber bamboos are controlled this way when they are planted to create a bamboo pass or passage garden—a grove of giant bamboo stems.

Once established, bamboos grow fast, completing vertical growth of 15 feet or more, depending on the species, in one to three months. For the first year a newly set out plant will send up a few stems. From about the second year on, more stems will appear and will grow higher, eventually reaching the ultimate height to which each particular kind grows.

Use the tall-growing kinds (golden bamboo is widely available, reaches about 20 feet) for screening. Plant near decks or engawas to tie house and garden together. Grow small clumps at one or two locations along a dry stream or behind a water basin arrangement.

Some kinds can be planted and trained as hedges. The low, dwarf bamboos, properly confined, also look good near water.

Use bamboo as a backdrop for a tall stone lantern, or plant it close to a window and keep the side branches pruned back so you can look out from the house into the garden through a thicket of stems.

TWO ALL-TIME FAVORITES for seasonal color in the Japanese garden are azalea (left), available in great variety of colors, and gardenia (right), which has white, highly fragrant flowers.

THE GROUND UNDERFOOT

Since the idea of a Japanese garden is to create a natural atmosphere, ground covers with irregular patterns and surfaces are generally preferred to lawns, which must be carefully groomed and therefore show more of the hand of man. Also, casual ground covers, such as moss, are more easily grown and maintained around the hills, mounds, and rock groupings that make up a Japanese garden.

The very low ground covers can require just as much care as a lawn. Though they may not need to be mowed, they have to frequently be cleaned of leaves. The deeper ground covers—ajuga, wild strawberry—have more of a natural look and though they need cutting back once in awhile their foliage hides fallen leaves.

Most ground covers will not hold up if they are continuously walked on; paths and stepping stones should carry most of the traffic in the garden. The Japanese often use gravel walks leading through low ground covers, or create graveled areas adjacent to large expanses of ground covers. The contrasts both in color and texture are quite pleasing.

If you have an existing lawn area, you can adapt it by creating earth mounds and planting them with a low ground cover that will visually blend in with the grass. Rock groupings with low shrubs or clumps of mondo grass will also help to break up the feeling of the flat plain created by a mowed lawn.

FLOWERING SHRUBS taller than about two feet are best used singly, so as not to overpower garden with too much color. At left is lilac (Syringa). On right is beauty bush, which has pink blossoms.

Planting Ground Covers

Late fall or early spring is the preferred season for putting in ground covers because plants can begin their job of covering the ground almost as soon as they're set out. Open spaces where weed seeds take hold are thus covered much faster.

The ground should be cultivated by working in generous amounts of organic matter: nitrogen-enriched sawdust, peat moss, leaf mold, ground bark. Rake to remove clods and stones, and water deeply for several days before planting.

If you're planting a steep bank, rake the cultivated soil crosswise, not up and down, to help prevent washouts. Water with a fine spray, starting at the bottom and working toward the top. If water starts to run down, stop spraying until the surface water soaks in.

Most nurseries carry ground cover plants in flats, pots, and cans. If you have a large area to cover, buy a flat or two. Depending on the plant, you generally cut the flat into squares about two inches on a side and set the squares out about 6 to 8 inches apart. The closer you space them the sooner the area will be completely covered.

Once your ground cover closes in and starts spreading, keep an eye on it so it won't overgrow stepping stones or ornamental rocks. Stones look more a part of the earth if a low ground cover is allowed to grow up around some of their base where it rests in the soil, but don't let them be hidden or they'll no longer look like stones.

After Irish moss has been growing well for a year or so, it may tend to lump up on itself and form mounds. If you don't like the looks of these hummocks, cut a 1-inch strip out of each and flatten the lump by stepping on it. The cut edges will be imperceptible and you can use the cut-out parts for planting new areas.

What are Good Ground Covers?

Except for large open areas that are bare of stones or other plantings, ivy is not too desirable a ground cover for a small garden. It gets too deep, spreads too fast, and most kinds have leaves that are too large for the compact feeling desired in the Japanese garden.

Of the subshrubs (shrublike but low growing) suitable for a small garden, ajuga is a good choice

---

 How to Make a Wet Garden

In nature you rarely see a marshy meadow or forest bog that isn't crowded with plants. A bog garden is an intermediate stage between a well drained, cultivated area and a garden pool. Many Japanese gardens have a large, constantly wet area that is not quite a pond or lake but contains moisture loving plants that create their own center of interest within the garden. Some gardens of this kind have stepping stones or bridges through the wet area to enable visitors to stroll over it while enjoying plantings of iris or lilies.

If your garden contains a section where water accumulates and stands even in summer, and if the soil and water are not too alkaline, you can develop a spot as a natural catch basin to drain water from the surrounding area and also to grow moisture loving plants.

Clear the area of weeds and grass. Spade the ground, incorporating generous amounts of humus such as sawdust, ground bark, peat moss, or compost. If the ground is too wet for digging, spread humus on the swampy ground; it will absorb water and eventually work down into the ground.

AN ARTIFICIAL BOG GARDEN. If you have an area that is wet for most of the year but dries out during later summer months, or if you just don't have a swampy spot, you can make an artificial bog garden.

Choose a low place to which drainage naturally flows. Mark out an area and dig it out to a depth of close to 3 feet. Line the hole with about 3 inches of concrete, using chicken wire for reinforcing. When the concrete is dry fill the basin with loose humus containing plenty of peat moss or compost.

You can supply water for an artificial bog garden by running a small pipe to it underground, or you can just fill the basin when the water level drops through evaporation. Install an overflow pipe just below the top to carry off excess water in rainy weather. Cover the outlet with a piece of hardware cloth to keep out leaves.

WHAT TO PLANT. *Trees:* Alder, bald cypress, birch, quaking aspen, willows. *Shrubs:* Bamboo, bog kalmia, hydrangea, red twig dogwood. *Perennials:* Calla lily, fern, Japanese iris, marsh marigold, plantain lily, Siberian iris.

RICH GROUND COVER of dichondra makes stepping stones look as if they were sinking out of sight. Major display on mound contains mondo grass, junipers, nandina, fatsia, pine, mahonia.

for an Oriental feeling. It will take sun or shade, but since it grows 4 to 6 inches high it should be cut back when it threatens to cover paths. Redwood sorrel *(Oxalis oregana)* has velvety green leaves on stems 2 to 10 inches high. It is a good ground cover for deep shade in the Pacific Northwest but it can spread aggressively.

Ice plant and other succulents seldom look as though they belong in a Japanese garden. The same can be said for ivy geranium.

The ideal ground cover for an Oriental garden is true moss, the kind you see growing on tree trunks or in deep shade in humid forests. However, true mosses require heavy shade and constant moisture. Also, they spread ever so slowly. If you live in a rainy area and natural moss is plentiful on trees and rocks, you might try transplanting some to your garden. Use a spatula or wide-bladed knife to lift off large strips, then press them into place on the soil at the base of rocks. Keep the moss damp and there's a good chance it will take hold and spread. (Page 67 gives information on cultivating your own moss.)

The next best choices are the close-cropped ground covers that will hug the ground and fill in between stepping stones. Mother-of-thyme, woolly thyme, chamomile, dichondra, baby's tears, Irish moss, and Scotch moss all require a minimum of trimming. Some of these will stand limited foot traffic; some take full sun, others need shade. All will give a low-lying carpet approaching true moss in its visual appearance.

SCOTCH MOSS, when newly planted in small squares, makes an interesting pattern. In time it will grow together, then mound up on itself. Though not true moss, it has a rich, velvety texture.

PLANTINGS AROUND WATER

Plants around a waterfall should generally be low and out-reaching; tall vertical forms tend to draw attention away from the cascade. Most ferns look good near water and should be planted close to it. Light, lacy foliage, such as a single branch of a Japanese maple, can be trained to reach out in front of a waterfall or over a stream to blend in with the rest of the garden.

Make use of the beauty of reflections by locating a lantern or an interestingly shaped dwarf tree at the edge of a pond where it will be mirrored in the water. Many gardens in Japan have been planned around a pond that gives a reflected view of Mount Fuji or the rising moon.

A most pleasant sight is that of flower petals dropping from a flowering fruit tree and floating on water. A tree branch can lean close to the surface, just touching it, so that the slightest breeze will cause it to dip into the water and cause ripples.

Almost any type of bamboo looks good in the company of water.

Natural ponds may cause you a little work in keeping them weed-free. You can thin out cattail, tule and other native reeds and rushes, then keep after the growth so it won't completely take over again. Like any other form of weeding, the first time is usually the worst...if this is any consolation. Some nurseries have chemicals that will help to keep natural growth under control.

A well-constructed pool or stream is fairly trouble free and little weeding is necessary.

There are several plant environments that result when you bring water into the garden. Each situation is usually suitable for plants.

■ Around the shoreline and just beyond. This area is good for plants that thrive in moist soil: Japanese elephant's ears, horsetail, water poppy,

True mosses have a velvetiness of texture and a range of rich colors that can't quite be matched by Irish or Scotch moss or baby's tears. You can't buy moss in a nursery but you can grow your own.

You need a nursery flat or shallow box, a roll of cheesecloth, a piece of insect screen, soil mix, and starter moss.

STARTING A CULTURE. To get a starter, look for natural moss on stones, on shingle roofs, or in shaded areas. Lift pieces with a penknife and dry them until they are crumbly. Remove the green part by scraping it away from the soil or crumbling the soil away. This fine, dry moss is your starter.

To keep soil from sifting out of a flat, cover any large openings in the bottom or sides with copper or plastic insect screen, or line with newspaper. If you use newspaper, make several slits at right angles to the bottom boards for drainage.

Fill the flat an inch deep with a good, fast-draining soil or prepared U.C. mix (50% fine sand, 50% peat moss or sawdust). If you use U.C. mix, soak with a solution of 1 part skim milk or prepared powdered milk to 7 parts water; the milk is a mild acidifier.

Cut two pieces of cheesecloth slightly larger than the flat. Place one piece on the soil surface and tuck in free edges between the soil and the sides of the flat. Sprinkle pulverized starter moss evenly over the cheesecloth, then place the second piece of cheesecloth over the starter and tuck in any loose edges.

Water gently but thoroughly; the cheesecloth should look wet but water shouldn't stand on the surface.

Place the sown flat in a shady spot out of wind and keep the soil moist, not waterlogged. Morning and late afternoon sun is sufficient for most mosses.

If the white color of the cheesecloth bothers you during the early stages of growth (it will eventually rot when you transfer the moss to its permanent location), place the cloth in a strong coffee solution (6 teaspoons instant coffee per cup of boiling water) for 10 minutes; remove and dry without rinsing.

USING WHAT YOU'VE GROWN. In two months the moss should have grown and penetrated both layers of cheesecloth; it will be just visible. In three months the moss will entirely conceal the cloth. After about 6 weeks you can grasp the cheesecloth at one edge and lift it, with the moss, out of the flat.

To fasten moss to a rock, mix equal parts of dry, crushed clay soil and sifted peat moss, then add enough water to make a putty-like material. Knead the mix until it handles easily. Plaster the mixture on a rock in a layer $1/8$ to $1/4$-inch thick, then fasten sheets of moss to it with short, hairpin-shaped copper wires.

Use the moss around the base of bonsai, between stepping stones, around or on rocks, on stone lanterns or water basins. It gives an aged, natural look that is hard to duplicate.

Most mosses grow best with morning and late afternoon sunlight, or in filtered shade. Some kinds thrive in full sun, greening up during rainy weather and lapsing into semidormancy when weather turns dry and warm. In the garden you can keep moss green by keeping soil reasonably moist. If it dries, it will revive when dampened.

MOSS STARTER is sown evenly on cheesecloth on top of soil, then second layer of cheesecloth goes over starter. In about 6 weeks, mossy sandwich can be cut with scissors and rolled up in strips.

LITTLE CARE is needed with ajuga ground cover, as long as drainage is good. Leaf colors are bronze, purple, or green.

water canna, Egyptian paper plant, creeping primrose, baby's tears, willow.

■ Under the surface of the water, where plants are almost entirely submerged. Recommended plants include water hawthorn, arrowhead, *Elodea, Valisneria,* eel grass, cabomba.

■ Floating on the surface. Water hyacinth, azolla, duck weed, water snowflake, water lettuce, ludwigia, parrot feather, anacharis.

Water lilies are the favorites of most water gardens. They come in many shapes, varieties, and colors, and in two main classes: hardy lilies, and tropical lilies.

Hardy lilies are easy to grow and have abundant and beautiful blooms. They die back with the first frost, winter safely (even under ice), and come back anew each spring. The tropicals make more demands on the gardener but produce blooms larger in size and in color range; almost all tropicals are fragrant. Except in those areas of the deep south and southwest that are safe for oranges, tropical lilies won't make it through the winter. In cold sections they must be treated as annuals—bought and planted in the spring, discarded in the fall.

A pool for water lilies should be 2 feet deep. They need about a foot of rich soil for their roots and a foot of water above that. They are best grown in underwater planting boxes.

Water hyacinth should be contained within a simple, floating wooden frame (use pine, not redwood), moored to the bottom of the pool with wire and a brick.

Lotus can be grown in a tub sunk under the surface of the water. Plant in fairly rich soil in the bottom of a half-barrel, cover with soil, and plant root stock in the soil, letting the growing tip stick out above the soil.

THE CARE OF YOUR GARDEN

The small Japanese garden is relatively easy to care for since there are no flower beds that require constant attention. Maintenance consists mainly of keeping the place neat and clean and periodically shaping plant forms.

As in any garden you should schedule an overall cleanup in the spring and in the fall. Do most of your deciduous shrub and tree pruning between late fall and early spring before the sap rises. If you plan to move an established plant or put in a new one, try to schedule the job for fall, especially if you live in a mild climate. It allows

FOUR WAYS to control form. Top left, supple branches weighted with rocks; lower left, wooden props supporting tree; top right, trunk wired to curved rod; lower right, trunk lashed to crossed stakes.

you to follow the heat, get ahead of the cold, take advantage of winter rains, and anticipate the spring growth surge. If you live where winters are cold, plant in the spring.

Throughout the year keep plant growth under control by nipping and pinching back young, tender growth.

Occasional cleanups keep your garden healthy as well as attractive. The more trash around the garden, the more breeding places there'll be for snails, slugs, earwigs, and other plant pests. If you keep pots or other plant containers in the garden, move them once in a while so you can check under them for pests.

Whenever you have a chance—even if you're strolling around enjoying the garden—pick off dead blossoms or pinch back new growth to direct it in the right direction. Once in a while make a tour to cut off dead wood, remove dead and dried foliage, and tie up any plants that need it. Keeping after the little chores prevents them

from growing into big ones. If you let the chores pile up, the garden may become more work than enjoyment.

Whenever you see a weed, pull it up. In a small garden it's better to remove weeds by hand; weed-killing chemicals can easily get to ground covers and shrubs.

Bamboo, heavenly bamboo, and most pines drop generous quantities of leaves. Though you won't want them scattered all over the garden, the leaves from such plants make a very good mulch. Spread them around the base of the plants to help hold moisture in the soil.

Clean up leaves and pine needles with a broom or bamboo rake (the bamboo type is more flexible and works better than the metal kind), but be careful not to tear ground covers by dragging a rake too hard. You can also use a jet of water from the hose, directed close to the ground.

Keep your garden clean, but don't make it look sterile. Remember that nature is not all apple-pie

BAMBOO LATTICE makes good support for plants such as wisteria (shown), ivy, jasmine, clematis, honeysuckle, Japanese hydrangea vine. Train foliage to cover, or leave open areas.

order. The classic story is told about the Japanese tea master who asked his young helper to clean the garden path. Several times the lad swept the path and picked up things, getting the garden neater each time, but still the master was not satisfied. Finally the master thrust the boy aside and shook a branch of a tree, sending a shower of autumn leaves onto the ground.

"There," he said, "that's nature's way to clean a path."

Where There's Water...

When it comes to watering, common sense is a pretty good guide, tempered by the remembrance that a Japanese garden is supposed to always look green, cool, and lush. That means that things should have plenty of water—should never be allowed to go dry.

If you are putting in a brand new garden, it's a good idea to include a sprinkler system that will cover the entire area. Short of such a convenience, you can locate small portable sprinklers in strategic places behind rocks or shrubs and connect them by a hose with multiple fittings. The hose can be buried a few inches beneath the surface or hidden under foliage.

Moss and ground covers are usually the first plants to show signs of too little water. They turn brown and crusty and unless taken care of will die out, leaving large bare patches. Soak large areas with a sprinkler early or late in the day, or use a canvas or plastic soaker that lets water escape slowly along its entire length.

Since your shrubs and trees will be mixed in

with ground covers or rocks, watering trenches will look altogether out of place unless you can conceal them. For watering deep-rooted plants—and this means almost anything other than ground cover—use a subsoil irrigator. This is a sharpened, perforated pipe that you attach to a hose then force into the ground near a tree or shrub to get water deep to the roots.

If you have a pond or pool in the garden, you'll inevitably have algae, which may be anything from a slippery coating of green on the bottom to a thick layer of scum on the surface. In a pool with no plants or fish, add a little household bleach or swimming-pool algaecide to keep the water crystal clear.

For a pool with plants and fish, there is a natural balance that will tend to cancel out much of the growth of algae. Just where that balance is must be determined for each case. Too many fish or too few plants will eventually result in too much algae. You can obtain—from fish breeders and nurseries dealing in aquatic plants—chemical preparations that keep algae down without harming other life. Or, you can resign yourself to periodically emptying and cleaning the pool.

Staking for Support

The Japanese use a wide variety of stakes, props, and supports for steadying young trees and for training branches of mature trees. Several of these devices are shown in photographs throughout this book.

A crutchlike prop, in the form of a tall, narrow letter "T," is used to support many trees that are trained to lean or arch and therefore need support to withstand wind or a mantle of winter snow. The props are usually made with natural poles rather than finished lumber— driven into the ground and bound together, and to the tree they support with rope or twine rather than wire (which would cut the bark), they become a part of the natural landscape.

Instead of using a single stake for a tree, drive a pair of short thick stakes into the ground on either side of a tree, well way from the trunk in order not to damage roots, angling them in toward the tree. Lash a cross-piece to the tops of the stakes, then lash the tree trunk to the cross piece.

Some vines have no way of holding on and ramble aimlessly on the ground unless you train and tie them. Many vines have built-in climbing devices—twining stems, or tendrils or rootlets along the stems. Tendrils or twining stems wrap around a support; these kinds of vines grow easily on trellises. Vines with disc-like tips or rootlets (such as Virginia creeper and several kinds of ivy) will grow against a wall or fence.

Instead of using a commercially made trellis for vines, make your own by tying bamboo poles together in a grid. Rope or twine will eventually weather to a darker color; if you want to hasten the aging process and make the lashings look more natural, dye rope by dipping it in a dark stain. Be sure it's completely dry before using it.

Moving a Small Tree or Shrub

If you are modifying an existing garden you may be faced with the prospect of either getting rid of an established tree or shrub or moving it to a new location. Unless a tree has grown to major size, transplanting is not the chore it may seem. (It is possible to transplant even fully grown trees but this is a job for a professional with experience and the proper equipment.) Try to schedule it during the cool season when the plant is dormant or semi-dormant.

Have the planting hole ready before lifting a plant out of its present location. Plants out of the ground should not be allowed to dry out or to freeze. Transplant the same day if possible; otherwise, keep plants in a shady, wind-protected place.

It's a good idea to cut the outer roots several months before transplanting by pushing a shovel down vertically as far as you can all around the drip line. This will help the plant to adjust to the shock of moving and will encourage the growth of fresh feeder roots close to the main stem. Two or three days before moving day, make a trench around the plant at the drip line and fill it with water every day. The water will help hold the soil in a firm ball for easier handling.

Decide on the size of root ball which will sever the fewest roots, then dig a trench around it. Shape the ball with light cuts using a spade or the back of a shovel. Cut down the sides of the trench to make room for undercutting and wrapping. Dig halfway under the root ball on one side, being careful not to crumble it.

Wrap burlap sacking around the ball as tightly as possible and pin the burlap together with large nails. Roll it underneath the cut half of the root ball. Undercut the other side of the hole, then lift the plant using a shovel as a lever. Place the plant on an open sack beside the hole and give it a final wrapping using heavy twine, starting at the base of the plant. Wrap upward to secure the entire ball, tying frequently to prevent slipping when the plant is moved.

In replanting, follow the procedure given for balled and burlapped plants on page 53.

USE	PLANT	REMARKS

	Coniferous evergreens (especially pine, fir, spruce, Japanese cryptomeria, cypress), oak, birch, larch	Use in background as stabilizing masses; in garden pruned to show form. Use to hide poor vista.
	Heavenly bamboo, true bamboos (especially tall-growing varieties	Train as hedge. Use single plants next to engawa or entry.
	Podocarpus, yew	Train as shrub or shrubby tree.
	Osmanthus, Mexican orange, natal plum, raphiolepis	Use as informal (untrimmed) hedge.

At or Near Boundaries

	Maple, oak, ginkgo, flowering plum, Japanese silk tree, mugho pine, dogwood, crape myrtle	Locate near base of hill, to one side, and train so branches will overhang mound.
	Juniper (most varieties)	Prune to display basic form.
	Azalea and rhododendron	Plant in mass to cover hill.
	Japanese aralia	Use behind or to one side of hill, because of large leaves.
	Mondo grass, blue fescue, dwarf bamboo, Korean grass	Use in clumps at points around base of hill, sides of mound. Restrict spreading bamboos.

Hills and Mounds

	Irish moss, baby's tears, true moss, Korean grass, Scotch moss, dichondra, ajuga	Not for traffic. Use between stepping stones and alongside paths among rocks.
	Mondo grass, ferns	Spot alongside path, among rocks.
	Dwarf bamboo	Use for path edging. Be sure to restrict spreading types.
	Star jasmine, low juniper (many varieties), thyme	Use alongside path; don't let overgrowth cover path but let spread in other directions.

On or Near Paths

in the Japanese Garden

USE	PLANT	REMARKS
 **Center of Interest**	Trees with autumn color (especially ginkgo, Japanese maple, Chinese pistache)	Use close to house, against fence, or against evergreen background.
	Pines (especially Monterey, Scotch, black, red, mugho, Jeffrey, Canary Island, jack, knobcone)	Plant single trees, prune and train to display basic form and character of structure.
	Flowering trees (especially plum, peach, cherry, almond, magnolia, dogwood, silk tree, goldenchain tree, golden trumpet tree)	Use against darker background, visible from house or special vantage point in garden.
	Timber bamboos	Be sure to restrict.
 **In or Around Water**	Astilbe, iris, fortnight lily, lily turf, Serbian bellflower	Use at water's edge (or along dry stream) for foliage and flowers.
	Sedges, bulrushes, papyrus, horsetail	Use in water at edges of pool and ponds. If not controlled, they will spread.
	Plantain lily	Use at edge of water in shade. Blossoms and large leaves.
	Mondo grass, dwarf bamboo, low-growing fern	Use adjacent to water basin or edge of pond. Control by thinning.
	Fatsia japonica, leopard plant, aspidistra, Japanese aucuba, heavenly bamboo, banana	Use adjacent to water basin or well. Interesting, luxuriant leaves.
	Fountain grass	Use in dry streams or dry ponds.
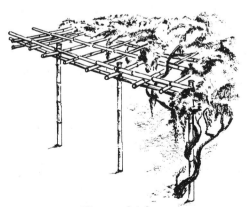 **Trellises and Arbors**	Wisteria, Mexican orange, clematis, actinidia, Easter lily vine, grape vine, morning glory, honeysuckle	Branches grow strong but they are easy to train when young. Train to cascade over lattice.
	Grape ivy, star jasmine, scarlet kadsura, natal plum	Train against fence, on arbors, or to spill over low walls.

FIRST GLIMPSE of this garden comes as you round curve of entry walk. The pond, stocked with rainbow trout, directs eye from lantern to lantern to Yoshino cherry. (Design, Nagao Sakurai.)

Water Creates Some New Dimensions

How to pretend with water…waterfalls, streams and running water…pools and fish…water basins…maintenance

Water, or the implication of water, is essential in a Japanese garden, whether it be a lake, a pond, a stream, or even a small trickle of moisture down the face of a rock. When it is impossible or impractical to have water—real, wet water—the Japanese suggest it by creating artificial stream beds and ponds, using stone in such a way as to hint that the dry condition is only momentary.

The beautiful dry garden of Ryoan-ji at Kyoto consists of only rocks and sand but the sand is raked to suggest a rippled sea around a series of islands.

Many classical Japanese gardens were originally created around natural bodies of water. There are "boating pond gardens," "cascade gardens," "lake gardens," and so on, depending on the way water is used. About the only type of garden that does not use water as a stream, lake, or pond is the tea garden. Nevertheless, the tea garden has a stone basin, which brims and overflows with water. Or, it may have a well, if only a symbolic one.

As with all other elements of the garden, water in whatever form you wish to use it should be part of a natural landscape or scene. Avoid tiled pools, brick edgings, metallic fountains—anything that indicates the hand of man rather than the result of nature.

Your decision to have water or no water will depend on how natural you want your garden, how difficult or expensive the addition will be, how much pleasure you will derive from its presence. Do keep in mind that the addition of water—the third element, along with plants and stones—means perhaps a little more of your involvement than either of the other two. Stones require no maintenance; plants can be kept up with only occasional attention; but water needs regular care, the amount depending on the amount of water.

On the plus side, water does some things that nothing else can:

■ Moving water adds real life to the garden. It sparkles and bubbles; it makes sounds; it has motion.

■ Water is a plastic, changing, decorative element. It responds to the slightest breeze and seems to become almost alive. It mirrors the sky and reflects images of objects around it.

■ Water makes the surrounding area seem cooler. If there is moving water in the form of a stream or spray from a falls, the effect is real—the air actually is cooled by evaporation. But even a small trickle of water over a stone or down the side of a basin refreshes the surroundings.

Many of the early gardens in Japan that were constructed around natural ponds and streams tried hard to repeat the surrounding topography. One garden in Kyoto, laid out in the year 794, was designed around a natural brook and pond to accommodate imperial boating parties. It was also the scene of the "feast of the winding stream," in which cups of wine were floated downstream. Guests seated along the banks picked up the cups and drank from them while composing poems.

It is perhaps unfortunate that less sybaritic times have fallen on us, and today it is rare indeed that a homeowner will be able to have a natural bit of water on his property. The city dweller or suburbanite must make do with the aid of plumbing and pumps or else be content with suggesting water.

NATURAL STREAMS

If yours is a rural setting with a natural body of water or a moving stream—short of the Western seasonal gulley washer—you may have your water and enjoy it too. However, a natural stream will seldom be precisely where you think it should be to enhance your garden. If you can't design your garden to accommodate the natural flow of water, you may have to divert it. Depending on the size of the stream, this may involve as little effort as digging a ditch that will allow you to tap off some of the main flow, or as much effort as bringing in heavy equipment to completely re-route the water course. If a stream happens to be in the right location, you may have to construct a partial dam to back up the water for a fall.

Make sure you are familiar with the moods of a natural stream. Many gently trickling brooks can become raging torrents during several days in winter.

Whatever tampering you contemplate, be sure to check out the legality of your plans. Often you may be able to simply reroute a brook that flows through your property, with no effect at all on property downstream; in effect you're just using the water as it flows by.

If the work involves any major changes—and damming is such a change—you would do well to consult with a professional who is familiar not only with the techniques but with the legal ramifications.

If a stream running through your property is used by spawning salmon, you must obtain permission from your state department of fish and game to alter it in any way. You may be required to construct a fish-ladder to compensate for changes that would block the passage of spawning fish or keep newly hatched fish from swimming to the sea.

A natural pond fed by winter drainage may be full in the winter but may drop in level or go dry altogether in the summer. There's little you can do to keep the level up in the dry months, since once the drainage supply stops the impounded water will start to evaporate. One answer, to keep the place from turning into an unsightly mudhole, is to build a cobblestone "beach" on a bed of concrete that will be exposed at low-water time. Of course, when the water does drop, much of the beach will have to be hosed free of muck, but once clean it will stay that way until the pond fills again the following winter.

If you have water in a small natural pond the year around, you might consider temporarily draining it and adding a cobbled bottom. Seldom will a pond have clear water, but by making it

 Ways to Suggest the Presence of Water

Hinting at water without actually using it—or using very little—is one of the more clever illusions characteristic of the Japanese garden. There are several ways this can be accomplished:

■ *The Dry Pond.* A shallow depression is scooped into the earth, then lined with smooth, flat stones (the larger the pond, the larger the stones). Or, fine gravel is used for filling in. Large rocks are used to simulate islands or stepping stones and are used along the edges to form a bank.

■ *The Dry Stream.* Light-colored, smooth, flat stones are used to line a shallow trench or stream

bed, or are simply spread out in a meandering course. Larger rocks along the edges, a wooden bridge, and plants such as iris, lily turf, blue fescue along the bank help the deception.

■ *The Empty Well.* A well border constructed of rough wood or stone, and merely sitting on the ground, hints at the possibility of water.

■ *The Wet Stone.* Even the tiniest trickle of moisture down a rock suggests that there might be more. A length of hidden tubing or pipe that connects with a hose outlet will let just a few drops run or drip onto a rock.

SUGGESTION OF WATER where none exists is successful in these three dry streams. Note how in smaller streams on the left the bed twists and bends in a most natural manner.

more shallow—through partial filling—and putting in a rock bottom, you can often keep the water clear enough to give you a pleasant view of the bottom.

Another possibility for a semi-wet area is a bog garden. See page 64 for hints on coping with a marshy area or creating one.

Keep natural settings natural. If you add rocks along a stream or at the banks of a pond, take your time with their placing. Study well the natural lay of the land and place new material to blend in with it, not contrast with it. If you expect to retain the natural look, don't edge a body of water with brick or even precisely placed stones. Vary the size of natural rocks; vary the contour; break up rock groupings with plantings that repeat varieties growing in the vicinity.

JUST PRETEND THERE'S WATER

In many Japanese art forms, some essential element of a composition is purposely left out in order that the observer can mentally provide the missing element. By participating in the composition the observer benefits more from its total meaning.

In the garden, water is often suggested without the actual use of water, and the viewer is able to become more a part of the garden, thus enjoying it more, by creating water in his imagination.

This is often done for esthetic purposes, but just as often for practical purposes. You can create the feeling of water in the garden without having either a natural source or special plumbing. This can be an advantage in a limited space.

Streams, waterfalls, and even ponds can be simulated without actual water. Use a grouping of rocks on a small hill or mound to suggest a waterfall—two large, rough boulders on either side of a lower, smooth rock. The height and the arrangement of the rocks will imply a hidden source of water and a cascade. To strengthen the illusion, use a tall rock with vertical striations or straight natural markings for the mirror stone (the one in the center) to give the effect of water running down its face. Construct the fall with as much care as you would if you were actually going to have water; the more real it looks, the better will be the illusion.

For a stream, plan a winding course through a portion of the garden, going from higher to lower ground, since water flows that way even in Japan. Use smooth, worn pebbles or gravel in the stream bed and larger rocks along the banks. Locate one

. . . HOW TO PRETEND

or more rocks along the edge to jut out into the "water," and place a low, worn rock in the stream. Mound up the pebbles slightly at the upper end of the large rocks that sit in the stream or project into it, much as moving water tends to pile up and form ripples where it encounters an obstruction.

The same general principles for building a dry stream apply to a dry pond. Use smooth pebbles for the pond, larger rocks along the banks. Make an island or two with low rocks. Make a beach with cobbles set close together and sloping into the make-believe water.

The effect of either quiet water or moving water can be created by taking the time to choose and arrange the bottom pebbles one by one. For a pond, use flat, circular stones and lay them close together to suggest still water. For a stream, use elongated stones and rather than just spreading them out at random, point each long axis in the direction that the stream is supposed to flow. This will suggest moving water.

Plant ferns in the ground at the edge of either a dry stream or dry pond. For an indoor garden, use potted ferns, concealing the container behind stones. Most of the low-growing bamboos look good, as do clumps of blue fescue, when planted among larger rocks along a bank or those used to form a waterfall.

Sprinkling a dry stream with the hose just before guests stroll through the garden makes it look even more realistic. Indoors, use a spray bottle to momentarily dampen the pebbles in a dry stream. You can also treat "water" pebbles in an indoor garden with a light coat of plastic spray (available in pressure cans at art supply stores) to give them a permanent sheen.

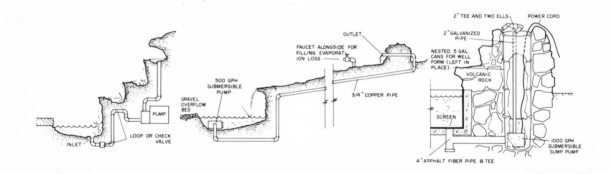

DRAWING shows scheme of waterfall with horizontal pump; waterfall with submersible pump; cascade waterfall. Photos at bottom show two different ways of feeding water into a garden pool.

In creating a dry stream or pond, keep these particular landscapes on a fairly limited scale. An artificial brook that twists and turns loses its effectiveness if it rambles all over the garden. If a dry pond is much larger than about 100 square feet, it will look like a real drought area.

WATERFALLS AND CASCADES

If there is water in your garden, you're missing half the pleasure if you can't hear it. Few sounds help to sooth your nerves like the soft splash of water.

Water can originate as a trickle over a rock or the edge of a basin, but if you have the facilities, why not utilize water to its fullest by having a falls feeding a stream or a pond?

The rock arrangement for a waterfall is given on page 88; the scheme is based on the traditional arrangement and is intended as a general guide. There are many possible variations, all in the realm of the "natural" garden.

Some Planning Tips

A cascade can fall over a rock in such a way that it drops in a threadlike line (like Yosemite's Bridal Veil Falls). It can pour evenly over a cliff-like rock in a broad sheet (like Niagara). It can divide on either side of a central rock (the water-dividing stone). The form of the water in the falls depends mainly on the shape and orientation of the rock it passes over in its vertical descent. A level, smooth-lipped rock will usually give a wide, sheetlike cascade. A roughly rounded lip will result in a tumbled cataract. A grooved lip can give a spouting effect that carries the water out and away from nearby rocks.

RIPPLES disturb reflecting surface of a quiet pool. Rocks around edge hide concrete, give pool natural look; in one section, turf curves over to meet the water. (Design, Noble Hoggson.)

WATER BASIN in traditional position near tea house, where soft trickling sound can be heard from within, and where it's handy to provide water for classical tea ceremony. (Design, George Kubota.)

. . . WATERFALL PLANNING

Scale is important. By keeping elements around a waterfall in the proper scale, a tiny volume of water can be made to resemble a busy torrent. Dwarf varieties of plants can be transformed by an active imagination into their full-sized counterparts, and small stones can be made to look as if they weighed hundreds of pounds. As a very rough rule of thumb, the smaller the total garden area is, the lower should be the height of a waterfall if it is to remain in scale. Whatever the total area, however, no waterfall should be lower than a foot in height or it will be insignificant. And unless you live in a naturally mountainous area and have an acre or so of terrain around you, 5 feet is about maximum for height. Anything over eye-level can become grotesque.

The farther water drops before hitting something, the more force it generates. The more force, the more the scouring action on whatever it lands. The floor of a pool that catches water should be made especially thick at this point to help absorb the wear. You can also use a layer of

gravel or loose rock here to break up the water as it hits. If falling water feeds a fish pond, have enough room for the fish to get away from the white water.

The face of a waterfall should be watertight. Otherwise, ground water will seep through, discoloring the flowing water. A stream bed or waterfall should have a concrete bed about 3 inches thick to prevent seepage.

Be sure to settle stone well in the ground or in concrete—particularly the larger rocks used in making a waterfall. Unless stones have a large part of their base firmly embedded, they look ready to tip over at any minute and may actually be unstable.

Pumps and Plumbing

The quickest way to get water is to let it run out of a tap. For more than a trickle, however, this can be expensive.

The mechanical heart of any waterfall using a significant amount of water is a pump, which is merely a set of whirling blades through which the water passes and by which it is pressured into further motion. A pump is driven by an electric motor, both put together as a single unit.

A pump can use the same water over and over. By recirculating it you don't waste it. Once a circulating system is set up and working—say from a waterfall to a stream to a pond, then back through a pipe to the waterfall again—you need only occasionally add water to replace that lost through evaporation.

A submersible pump can sit on the floor of a pool under the water, hidden by rocks, or it can be located in a masonry well at the base of the waterfall. Flexible tubing carries water from the pump to the source for the waterfall. Separate piping is used for filling and draining, or filling can be accomplished with the garden hose. The motors of submersible pumps are housed in watertight cases and never need lubricating. A submersible pump sucks water in from its immediate surroundings, then pushes it out to where it can be transformed into a feeder point for a waterfall or a hidden "spring" for a stream.

Fully submersible pumps range from tiny 1/55

horsepower models that can lift water to a height of 2 feet, to a husky unit that can lift water to a height of 12 feet. Costs for submersible pumps range from about $20 to $60.

Since submersible pumps work under water, they are completely silent.

Other pumps, with the motors exposed, are available in either horizontal or vertical models. One type pulls water along a level pipe from pool to pump, then pushes it upward. The other type sucks water up directly and keeps it going in the same direction. The vertical type is the more efficient but must rest in shallow water of a pool —usually 2 to 4 inches deep. This may require your building a special arm for the pool which you can disguise with stones or plantings.

The horizontal pump pushes water up more efficiently than it pulls it up, something to keep in mind when designing your water layout and locating the pump.

A horizontal pump can be placed almost anywhere outside a pool, and it is frequently the answer when the distance between pump and outlet is far.

 ## How to Frighten a Wild Boar

There's the venerable story of the man who lived in a large city and who daily donned a feathered costume and grotesque mask and performed a strange dance. Questioned as to the ritual, he replied that it was to keep tigers away from his house. When told that there were no tigers in that part of the world, he smugly answered, "See, it works."

You may not have wild boars (or tigers) in your garden, but the *sozu kakehi* is a device that might keep them away if you did. Though it's more fanciful than practical, it does make a good center of interest and is a charming way to handle water.

Water flows out of a length of bamboo into another which is closed at one end and pivoted in the middle. When the lower piece is filled, it tips, empties, then drops back, striking a rock with an audible "klonk."

THE SOZU KAKEHI is made from two lengths of large-diameter bamboo. The one that provides the water can be an open flume, as above, or it can be closed completely along its entire length.

For greatest efficiency, a pump should be installed to keep the distance it has to move the water as short as possible. Non-submersible types can be concealed with shrubbery or rocks. They do tend to be less quiet than the submersible type, so you'll have to get used to some mechanical noise. Any pump should be situated such that you can easily get to it if the need arises.

Electrical connections for a small recirculating pump can be as simple as plugging its waterproof cord into an outdoor outlet in the garden.

Always make sure you understand the manufacturer's directions for installing and operating a pump before you start one up.

Garden pumps and professional advice are available at garden equipment suppliers. Also, check the classified section of your telephone directory under "Pumps."

TO FILL A BASIN

A waterfall is perhaps the most dramatic way of introducing water into the garden. However, if space is a limitation, or if you prefer water to make a more peaceful entry, you may want to forego a cascade and start water moving on a smaller scale.

You might arrange a small outlet within a stone grouping to allow water to drip gently off the lip of a rock. Or you could have a thin stream run down the face of a rock. You might want to drill a hole through a chunk of lava rock that will allow water to seep through when fed from behind. By burying copper or plastic tubing under the stones of a stream bed you can have the effect of a stream welling up out of the ground.

A *kakehi* is a flume or pipe that brings water above ground level. It is most often used to supply water for a stone basin. Only a trickle is needed, so rather than installing a pump, water is supplied by running a pipe or tubing from a hose bib through the flume and controlling the flow with a faucet valve located at the hose bib or concealed somewhere near the flume.

The kakehi is usually not used to feed a stream directly, since it is a man-made object and therefore not a natural source of fresh water. However, a flume can run water into a basin whose overflow then becomes part of a small-scale stream or pool.

See page 139 for design details for several flumes, and page 136 for ideas on the classical Japanese water basin arrangement. Page 81 shows how to use water to create an interesting sound that will keep the garden free of badgers or wild boars—if such is your trouble.

CONSTRUCTING A STREAM

A stream carries water from one elevation to a lower level. Depending on the amount of water available, the length of the stream, and its slope, the water may flow gently and quietly or it may rush along, splashing and sparkling over rocks. To keep water in motion, the slope of any stream should be at least one inch in four.

Generally, streams should twist and wind since a straight stream of any length tends to look like a playground slide. But turns and bends need a reason for being, either a natural one or a created one. In laying out a stream, plan its course to follow the contours of the ground. Let it curve around mounds or trees; set a rock or shrub at the inside of some of the bends.

Base your layout on observance of nature. Water that moves casually wanders in curves, always scouring the outside bank of a curve. Thus, a stream should be wider and deeper at the mid-point of a curve, and shallower along the inside arc because silt precipitates in the eddies of the curve.

Fast water rushes in a fairly straight line, detouring only where rocks bar its path.

To plan a stream, lay out a rope in the general course you want the stream to take. Avoid sharp, unnatural bends, and remember that water flows downhill. Decide on the best shape for the stream from the best viewing point in the garden.

Be sure to integrate the layout with the rest of the garden. Start the stream from a logical point—a waterfall, a water basin, a simulated underground spring—and carry it to a logical point such as a pond. Don't have a stream spring full blown from under a fence and disappear as mysteriously under the wall of the house.

Once you have plotted the shape of the stream, dig the bed out to a depth of 8 to 12 inches, sloping the sides. There is no rule for width; it should be in scale with the total length of the stream as well as with the rest of the garden. To visualize the overall form better, lay out a pair of ropes, roughly parallel, to define the width as well as the configuration.

Next, line the stream bed with 3/4 inch of crushed rock to a depth of about 2 inches, then

POND in rear corner of a suburban lot is fed by 5-foot waterfall, out of picture to the left. Charming gravel beach curves and narrows, and is lost in the plantings behind the snow-viewing lantern.

apply a layer of fine gravel that will work down between the pieces of rock. Pack the stone down tightly by tamping it with the end of a sturdy length of lumber (a 5-foot piece of 4 by 4 or 4 by 6 works well). Instead of crushed rock and gravel you can lay wire fencing (2-inch mesh) right on the ground for reinforcing.

Pour in 2 inches of concrete, working it into the base rocks or wire, and troweling it up the sides. If you want to leave bare concrete for the bed, roughen the surface with a stiff broom after it has started to set up. This will help to disguise the artificial look of the concrete. Better yet, press wet, round pebbles at least 1 inch in diameter into the concrete while it is still soft to form a more natural looking stream. Or, sprinkle concrete mix over the damp concrete.

Set larger rocks in the concrete along the edges or in the center.

Cover the stream with sacks or heavy rags and keep them damp for about 24 hours before running water through it. The concrete should be well cured, or flowing water may loosen the stones.

The finished stream will have a depth of about 3 to 7 inches, depending on how deep you dug the original trench. Anything deeper than that will require too much water; anything shallower will seem skimpy. A stream bed does not have to be full to the top.

You can build in an occasional eddy by flattening out the bottom of the stream in one or two places or by making the depth greater at a chosen spot. If you let some of the edging stones project into the stream, they will cause ripples. Small islands formed with jagged rocks will create rapids and rough water that both looks and sounds pleasant.

POOLS AND PONDS

Water can take many forms in the garden and most of the forms can be used individually or together. For example, a water basin can be just that: water drips from a flume into the basin,

LICHEN-COVERED ROCKS conceal copper pipe, barely visible, where stream originates. Ferns and azaleas thrive in cool, moist spot. Stream planted with fern, lily turf. (Design, Tatsuo Ishimoto.)

MAJOR-SIZED STREAM splashes along several cataracts formed by stepped-down series of smooth rocks. At this point the water course is about three feet across, only inches deep.

overflows, and disappears into the ground. Or, a basin can be a part of a complex whereby the overflow feeds a small pond, which in turn feeds a small waterfall that courses into a stream bed.

A stream can have its own reason for being or it can drain into a pool. A pool can sit by itself or it can be fed by a stream or directly by a waterfall. About the only water element that must have another element along with it is a waterfall. A waterfall can rise from a simulated hidden spring, but a waterfall has to go somewhere.

An enclosed body of water, such as a pond, can sit by itself in the garden but if a pond can be made to look more than having recently dropped out of the sky, it will give the garden much more vitality. Its inlet may be a stream or waterfall, or an imaginary spring. Its outlet may be a stream or waterfall, or even a simulated seepage of rocks and vegetation.

Many of the ancient gardens in Japan contained small-scale lakes or were built around natural ponds large enough to accommodate a boat. Some had islands, connected to the mainland by bridges. A few of these have been preserved as national shrines or public parks, but gardens built today seldom have room for a lake. Ponds or pools are more practical, especially for the Westerner, and if designed with care can give the same effect of a peaceful body of still water.

Whatever the shape of a pond, its outline should not be clearly visible. Even a natural pond can be blended in with its surroundings by adding groups of rocks and clusters of plants near the water's edge. Seldom will either stones or plants by themselves do the job—you need both.

Constructing a Small Pool

Small pools can be easily made by digging a hole and sinking a water-tight container into the ground. Old laundry tubs, oil drums, wine barrels, darkroom trays, Chinese *woks* (frying pans), water tank ends, or half-tanks are a quick and simple answer for a limited space. Leave about an inch of rim above ground to keep soil from washing into the pool. Since such pools are small, their overflow can usually just seep into the ground.

The Chinese wok makes a good pool for an indoor garden. Stabilize it well so there's no

BACKDROP TO POOL is provided by weeping cherry, birch tree. Fern, juniper, grasses edge stream and pool, softening rock edging. At right, fencing forms arch over which foliage is trained.

... SMALL POOLS

chance of it being tipped when full of water, and hide the edges with stones and potted plants. Change the water periodically to keep it clean and fresh, or rig up a miniature waterfall and recirculating system using a submersible pump.

To conceal the bottom of a tank-pool paint it black or arrange a close pattern of pebbles over it.

Small pools of this type have limitations. They can be ill-suited to keeping fish or water plants which must be thinned regularly to avoid overcrowding. The small amount of water in them can change temperature too fast for the health of either. Such pools work best in a small garden where they can serve as miniature reflecting pools. Place small pools in secluded corners where they can become a very special part of a garden, or close to a path where they can be enjoyed in passing.

Be careful about locating a small pool right at the end of a path. One homeowner had to reroute a path that had been designed to terminate with a tiny pool that was the same size as the stepping stones. Too many guests would take a step from the last stone directly into the pool!

The next step up in size and permanence, before getting into the concrete pool, is a plastic pool kit offered by some pump manufacturers. A heavy-gage sheet of plastic is included with a submersible pump. You dig a hole, spread the plastic over it, fill with water, place the pump in the pool, and arrange stones and plants around the edges. Another choice is reinforced fiberglass. Such pools are prefabricated or you can buy the raw materials and make your own.

Constructing a Moderate-Sized Pool

Most pools on a fairly modest scale can be built around a shallow, concrete shell. First, lay out the general form of the pool, using a garden hose or rope to define its limits. Dig a sloping depression about a foot deep at the lowest point. (Straight sides that are squared off with the bottom make corners that are tough to keep clean.) Dig trenches and install plumbing for a drain, if you want to make emptying the pool easier; without a drain you'll have to siphon or pump out the water for cleaning. Cover the drain pipes with soil, and line the hole with about 2 inches of ³/₄-inch crushed rock followed by fine gravel, and tamp it all down.

Concrete could be poured right into the base hole on top of the raw earth, but the compacted gravel minimizes possible cracking of the shell by settling soil, particularly in cold-weather areas where soil freezes and thaws.

If you wish, reinforce the bottom by spreading wire fencing or heavy chicken wire over the gravel.

STILL WATER OF POND mirrors trees, shrubs growing along edge; since end of pond is distant from inlet, ripples are caused by wind or fish. At right, Japanese iris give dramatic effect.

Next, pour in 4 or 5 inches of concrete. The mix shouldn't be too wet or you won't be able to trowel it up the sides. Make the pour in one continuous operation, so there will be no joints for water to seep through, troweling the mix to a rough surface when everything is poured.

For a natural effect, set a mosaic of round pebbles (pre-soaked in water) in the concrete while it's still soft. Keep the pool shell covered and damp for a couple of days before filling it. The longer and slower you let the concrete set—especially in hot weather—the harder it will be.

Be sure there is a raised lip all around, slightly higher than grade, to keep surface water out during heavy rains.

One side of the pool can be sloped more gradually than the others and paved with cobbles or rubble to make a beach.

Curing is necessary for a pool that is to contain plants or fish. Fill the new pool with water and let it sit for 24 hours. Drain, refill, and repeat three or four times. The last time, let the water stand for a week, then rinse the pool thoroughly and refill. Then you can add fish or plants.

You can construct a garden pool up to about 500 square feet by these methods, though anything larger than about 250 square feet should be reinforced with steel rod rather than wire. For a project much larger you'll be better off getting professional help. Digging a hole to accommodate a really major-sized pool is best done with mechanical aids.

In addition to using rock around the perimeter of a pool you can use wood posts or stakes in one area to form a series of miniature pilings. Use various lengths of oak, cedar, juniper, or other coniferous wood (but not redwood, which will stain concrete and water) in diameters ranging from 2 to 6 inches. Leave the bark on for a more natural appearance. Set the lengths vertical and butted tightly against one another, but not aligned in a smooth arc, embedding the bottom ends in concrete at the same time you pour the main shell for the pool. The bottom ends should rest completely in concrete, not on bare ground, to a depth of 4 inches or more. Pour a thin shell of concrete behind the pilings to back them up.

If You Have Goldfish . . .

The depth of a pool with fish should be at least three times the length of an adult fish, in at least one area of the pool.

Carp and large goldfish are often kept in Japanese gardens, both of them having symbolic importance as well as visual interest. The two species should be separated from each other by being in separate pools or by a division within a single pool (underwater screen or glass), since goldfish will eat carp eggs.

In many parts of the country raccoons, skunks, and other nocturnal animals will stake out a fish-filled pool and make periodic raids. If any fish

LAYING OUT THE WATER COURSE. Plan your layout of falls, stream, or pond carefully; once the project is completed, making changes in height or direction will be difficult. A waterfall or series of cascades must have plenty of vertical fall—a minimum height is about 3 feet. (This doesn't mean the water drops that distance all at once; the drop may be used up over a horizontal distance of 30 feet.)

Lay out the water course from the highest point in the garden to the lowest point using a length of rope or hose, making graceful bends and curves. Once you're happy with the basic pattern, install the necessary plumbing and establish the point of the main fall at the very top, the pond (if you plan one) at the very end, and any intermediate cascades. Don't line up the source waterfall and the cascades but stagger them laterally to give the configuration added visual interest.

CONSTRUCTING THE FALLS. Now make a selection of the primary or main rocks that will form the waterfall, the cascades, and bends in the stream, remembering that these points require larger rocks than those used along the way. Set the stones roughly in place, leaving fine adjustments for later.

The toughest part of the whole project is getting the big rocks of the main falls into place, and you may need help. Dig out beds for those primary rocks and settle them firmly in the soil. (You may want to wire large rocks together temporarily if they seem unsteady.) The general pattern is two large stones flanking the falls and leaning slightly in, toward each other. Between the flanking stones, and somewhat behind them, is a rock called the mirror stone—it's the stone that the water flows over. Water can originate from a small

pool behind the mirror stone or can just flow out of plumbing and down the mirror stone, however you choose.

At the base of the fall dig out a pool or a stream bed, compact the soil and wet it, and lay down wire fencing for reinforcing. Start filling in with concrete of a slurpy consistency, a shovel at a time, banking it higher at the back and sides. Set secondary stones at the edges, settling them into the concrete. Leave pockets behind the secondary stones to be filled in with loose soil for planting.

Now fill in around the secondary stones with smaller stones, adding more if needed. Use a stiff, wet paintbrush for final troweling—it's easier to get into tight corners than a regular trowel.

Don't try to pour all the concrete at once but work at a couple of square feet at a time. (Large pools are an exception. You must make the pour all at once. Only after pouring and troweling the bottom should you set the edge stones and mortar.) When all rocks are in place, including those along the edges, fill in the pool area with concrete and use a metal trowel to get the bottom flat. As you work, keep checking to see that you retain a slope from back to front.

If you plan a series of cascades, carry reinforcing wire over the slope formed in the earth. Work the concrete in the upper pool right up to the edge, then pour the back edge of the lower pool and build the concrete up to join the other.

After you've troweled the pool or stream beds, and while the concrete is still wet, sprinkle dry concrete mix or soil over the wet concrete. It helps to hold moisture and also gives the finished appearance of a natural bottom.

For at least 24 hours keep fresh concrete covered with sheet plastic or damp burlap and don't run water over it.

PRIMARY ROCKS FOR A WATERFALL are set in place first and then backfilled with earth. At center, the large secondary stones are mortared in. Finally, pool area is filled, edges troweled with wet brush.

COMPLETED WATERFALL and stream shown under construction on facing page. Series of cataracts and rocks in midstream bring water alive as it flows along. (Designer, Toshio Saburomaru.)

survive those attacks, they may fall prey to neighborhood cats. To protect your fish from predators, sink several good-sized stones beneath the surface, arranging them to make small protective caves in which the fish can hide. Volcanic rock works well; you can gouge holes into it and submerge pieces several inches under water.

You can also protect fish by putting a layer of fine-mesh chicken wire between them and the surface. The one drawback is that the wire will usually be visible.

MAINTENANCE

Most garden pools need a thorough cleaning every two or three years. By then water plants will have collected on the bottom and algae on the sunny sides of a pool. In windy or dusty areas a yearly cleanup may be in order.

If you have fish in a pool, remove them as well as any snails and carefully place them in a large bucket filled with water from the pool. Drain the pool and remove all plants and plant containers.

Scrub grime and algae off the bottom and sides with a stiff brush and water. You can use soap if you rinse the pool several times afterwards. A good blast of water from a hose helps to flush out dirt.

Check for cracks and leaks. Clean them out and fill and cover them with a ribbon of patching cement.

Replace plant material and refill the pool, but wait a day before you put the fish back in. Fish don't like sudden temperature changes, so don't just dump them into the new water. Set the bucket containing them in the pool for a few hours until the water temperatures are about the same. Then tilt the container and let the fish swim out of it into the pool.

Streams generally need less cleaning than a pool, since moving water helps to carry dirt along. When a stream begins to look grimy turn off the water and then scrub the bottom with a stiff brush. If the stream feeds a pool containing fish, you'll have to clean the whole works unless you can block the stream to treat it separately.

Mosquitoes create a nuisance in still water; however, mosquito fish *(Gambus affinia)* thrive on their larva. Though they aren't very showy, the fish do a good job in keeping the insect population down. They are less than a couple of inches long and can wiggle through very shallow water. Check with aquarium supply stores or your country mosquito abatement department.

Aside from periodic cleanings, pick dead leaves and twigs out of the water and keep an eye on fish and plant life to make sure it's healthy.

STEPPING STONES that bridge water must be large enough, flat enough, and close enough that even a small child can cross over without having to risk hopping from one to the other.

Paths and Walks in Your Garden

Classical stone paths...paving...the most natural paths...the sound of gravel underfoot...steps up and down...bridges

A path is much more than a way to get from one place to another place. Like so many of the elements in the Japanese garden, a path is intended to be an experience as well as a means to enjoying the entire garden.

For a path to be a pleasure in itself, materials are used that add one more contact with nature—materials such as natural stone, gravel, wood, earth. Concrete and asphalt are rarely used except in large public gardens that must accommodate a great deal of foot traffic. Also, materials are chosen for their tactile value to give a pleasant feeling underfoot, or for the sound they make when walked on.

Strolling along a path in a Japanese garden is an exciting adventure. Rarely does a path lead directly to a destination. There is usually an intriguing curve that makes you take an extra step or two but rewards you with a special view.

The Japanese design their garden paths for

casual wandering, with frequent stops to permit you to inspect things along the way or enjoy a patch of cool shade. Paths are longer than the shortest distance between two points. Even in small areas paths are designed to ramble. By going the long way around you get the feeling that a garden is larger than it actually is.

Nevertheless, a path is also utilitarian. It is intended to guide you around and through the garden. Thus, a path should go from somewhere to somewhere. It should begin at a gate or some entry to the garden and it should end at the house, or at a water basin, or at the edge of a pond. A path that starts from nowhere is a deception, and one that ends abruptly with no reason is a disappointment. If designed properly, a stream can appear and disappear, since that is the nature of water, but a path must serve its purpose of guiding traffic.

A path should keep foot traffic out of certain places in the garden—planted areas or stone groupings—but should not appear to confine the stroller. The trick is to keep people on a path while still making the garden look as if it is open. There should be definite boundaries to a path, but they should be low or irregular enough that they don't appear severely restrictive.

One way to avoid a confined look is to vary the path border. If you plant a hedge along one portion, use stone to edge another section. A stretch of low, open fence might give way to a mound of earth with a stone lantern. Train a grove of bamboo or birch trees along one side of a path and perhaps run a stream bed along the other side.

A good path guides foot traffic through the garden without appearing to do so. It is natural in its appearance and adds to the beauty of the garden without detracting from it. A random arrangement of flat stones or a large area of gravel with no apparent direction can be confusing.

THREE KINDS OF PATHS

There are three general kinds of garden paths. No one is "better" than any other; the choice of which to use depends on your particular situation. Often, more than one kind of path can be used in the same garden.

■ *Natural paths* are the kind of footpath created by people and by animals following the same route until the ground is packed and clear of growth. Except in a very big garden that is purposely kept in a wild state, a natural path needs some help from the hand of man to keep it from looking unkempt. Weeds must be controlled and the path must be clearly defined by surfacing it with gravel, bark, pine needles, or such materials.

Where the soil dries slowly in spring, a 4 to 6 inch layer of sawdust or firbark makes a good natural path. These materials need renewing annually but as they gradually break down they improve the soil.

■ *Stone paths* are perhaps the most common kind of path used in a Japanese garden. At its simplest a stone path is a series of flat rocks arranged in such a way that you can easily step from one to another. A stepping stone path is fairly easy to design and build, and materials are readily available almost anywhere. When skillfully laid out, stepping stones can look as if they had always been there. Stepping stones can be used almost any place in a garden, even to extend a path across a pond or stream.

Freezing temperatures can make stepping stones and even paved paths hazardous. For safety, scatter a little sand over icy paths; it'll help keep you from slipping and in warm weather any leftover can be swept off. (Don't use salt or ashes; either one will leach into the surrounding soil and may harm plantings.)

■ *Paved paths* can range from irregular designs in flat stones laid closely together to regular shapes of cast concrete. A paved path might be brick, or even asphalt or concrete, though these are usually too tailored for the family type of Japanese garden. Paved paths are a little more formal in feeling than stepping stones but sometimes they work well with the more formal architecture of the West. Paved paths require a degree of construction skill, especially if you want a tight-fitting configuration that includes both natural and man-made stone.

In dry climates or sunny locations paved paths are neat and easy to walk on. If they are wet a great deal of the time they may become slippery with moss. Though moss adds to the natural feeling, you may want to keep it under control by

PASSAGE GARDEN leads between house and fence to tea garden. Stepping stones are ideal in narrow space, where paving would be formal.

PAVING OF CLOSE-SET concrete blocks is made less formal by irregular stones set randomly and flush with the surface.

NOTE CONTRAST between these massive, rough-edged stepping stones and precise, geometric path in top photo.

periodically scraping the thickest growths or using a wire brush to clean off thin growth.

As a rough guide, use the more formal arrangements of paved paths near the house. Within the garden use stepping stones or open paving, and near the edges of the garden use natural paths.

Stepping stones and open paving serve you well for foot traffic but may pose problems if you have to move a wheelbarrow or mower around the garden. If the need for such equipment is infrequent, you can lay boards over stepping stones, or even over most low ground covers, to serve as a temporary path for wheels.

STONE PATHS ARE CLASSICAL

Some early Japanese writings on classical gardens laid down strict rules for the placement of stepping stones and even specified heights that reflected one's station in life. Stepping stones that the Emperor walked on were supposed to be no less than six inches high; the Samurai (warrior class) rated stones three inches high; for commoners, an inch and a half sufficed.

It is unclear whether this is a commentary on who was able to derive the most pleasure from a garden, but it would seem that the lower the stone, the easier the walking and thus the more the enjoyment.

Stepping stones can be natural rocks with a flat surface; they can be cast forms; they can be combinations of the two. Some path designs in older gardens have even made use of old mill stones, slabs of granite from walks, or bits of stone piers from demolished bridges. Such materials are not readily available today, but you may occasionally come across lengths of granite once used for street curbs that can be worked into a path or used for a small bridge.

Almost any flat-topped rock can be used for stepping stones provided the individual stones are large enough to accommodate a person's foot.

A Variety of Forms and Types

Even when two points that are to be connected by a path are close together and opposite one another, it is better to curve a path or angle it rather than extend it arrow-straight. For example, if your house entry is directly opposite a gate opening into the garden, route the connecting path around a rock arrangement or planting, or angle it one way and then another before it reaches its goal. This will give more depth to the garden and make the trip between gate and house more interesting by building into it an air of anticipation.

...STONE PATHS

A path should make you want to linger along the way instead of hurrying you on to the end. This is why a straight path is less appealing than one that wanders. Furthermore, a straight path tends to divide an area, making it appear smaller than it actually is. Design paths to wander among trees, under branches, around a large rock. The more variation you create, the more interesting the garden will be.

As much as space in the garden permits, turns in a path should be smooth rather than abrupt. Sharp turns are like sharp rocks in that they introduce a feeling of disquiet. Paths with angled turns are more formal in feeling than those with smooth curves. It's best not to mix the two types in the same garden.

Any path must have a recognizable unity. Loosely scattered stones with no linking theme are confusing to the eye.

A path of stepping stones can be made up of individual stones large enough to walk on, spaced and arranged for comfortable walking, or such primary stones can form a basic framework to which you then add smaller, secondary stones. The primary stones carry most of the traffic while the small ones are ornamental and help to visually stabilize the others.

Primary stones arranged in a straight line are difficult to walk on. Try to locate stones for an average length of a person's step so strolling the path can be done without giant-sized strides or mincing little steps. Stepping stones in older gardens in Japan are spaced just a few inches apart to accommodate the dainty steps of ladies who once wore tight robes and teetering clogs.

MONOTONY OF LONG PATH is broken by using old stones in various sizes and shapes, by water channel suggesting river across path. This is a narrow side yard—just five years old—in Tokyo.

Twelve Stone Path Arrangements

FORMAL PAVING	STEPPING STONES	MISCELLANEOUS
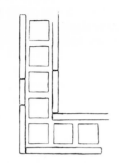		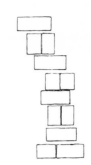
CONCRETE BLOCK	*PRIMARY STONES*	*DOUBLE-SINGLE BLOCK*
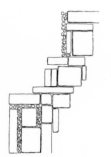		
BLOCK & GRAVEL	*PRIMARY, SECONDARY STONES*	*BLOCK, STONE, GRAVEL*
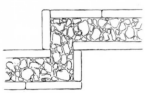	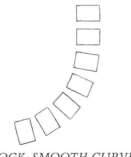	
STONE, BLOCK EDGE	*BLOCK, SMOOTH CURVE*	*STRAIGHT-SIDED STONE*
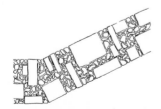	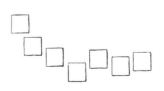	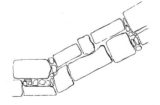
TIGHT BLOCK-STONE	*BLOCK, IRREGULAR CURVE*	*LARGE STONE, GRAVEL*

As long as the primary stones are large enough to step on comfortably, say, 8 to 14 inches in diameter, the distance between them can be about 4 to 6 inches. This is somewhat less than an average stride but it induces a person to linger.

Planning Stone Paths

Here are some hints to guide you in planning a stone path:

■ Space stones for easy passage from one to another. Remember that people of different ages and different strides will be using them. There is no one standard step. The farther apart stones are, the more difficult they will be to walk on in wet or frosty weather.

■ To establish a flowing continuity in a path, select each stone so it relates in shape to the next one. You can combine irregularly shaped stepping stones with stone blocks or man-made stepping stones, but it takes skillful arranging to blend the two. Some of the photographs in this book show such successful combinations; study them to gain a feeling for using both shapes.

■ Use stones large enough to accommodate the foot comfortably but not so large that you have to hop from one stone to another. Within limits, the larger the stone the more stable and permanent it looks. Don't have all stones in a path the same size but vary them enough to add interest while still keeping them working harmoniously together.

■ Use a larger stone at an intersection in a path,

LEISURELY WALKING on this path—and being led by it—is part of the pleasure of a Japanese garden. Since you walk only on the stones, the surface of the gravel remains smooth and undisturbed.

WHAT COULD BE more inviting than a path that almost imperceptably becomes a series of steps leading you to a higher level, then around a mysterious corner of the garden! (Design, F. H. Mick.)

at a junction of two branches of a path, at a definite curve, or at any place a stroller might pause for a moment. If a path curves past a special viewpoint, a large stepping stone invites you to stop.

■ In most cases lay stones broadside across the path rather than lengthwise to it. A path made up of stones all arranged with their longest dimension in the direction of the path seems to hurry you along. A path whose stones have their longest dimension perpendicular to the axis of the path seems more a series of steps than a quick route through the garden. Also, it's much easier to design' curves when primary stones stretch across the path instead of along it.

■ Be sure to set stepping stones firmly. At least two-thirds of the stone should be buried for stability. It's disconcerting to step on a stone that moves underfoot. (See later pages in this chapter for information on setting stepping stones.)

■ Set each stone so its surface is level. The base of a stepping stone can be rough, since it is buried, but the top should be reasonably flat.

Flagstone...Rock of Ages

Flagstone—or turfstones, as they are also called—represent a significant investment but a very good investment. A flagstone path, whether you like a paved one or stepping stones, is as solid and durable as it looks; indeed, if properly constructed it can last forever.

You can choose among several different types of flagstone. Two are especially popular for a Japanese garden: Arizona flagstone is usually

THIS IS VIEW of the approach to the stone steps shown on page 97. Lantern, edge of pond, and large rock at right form turning point for path and induce stroller to pause for a moment or two.

. . . FLAGSTONE

available in either irregular or rectangular slabs, from 1/2 to 2 inches thick. Arizona flagstone varies in color from pink to sandy to gray, any of these colors usually being mottled with white. It is a little too formal looking for stepping stones, unless you plant low ground cover around it to soften the sharp edges. This type of flagstone sometimes has a tendency to flake apart, and it's best set in a bed of sand or concrete. It's fairly easy to cut on the job and can be used effectively in a paving configuration in combination with other types of stone.

Water-washed flagstones are relatively smooth with rounded edges, are gray in color, and may be as much as 6 inches thick. They are best for informal paths. This type makes a handsome stepping stone when most of its bulk is buried in the earth. Use very large stones (4 or 5 feet long by 2 or 3 feet wide) for shoe-removal stones at a house entry. Rather than attempting to cut water-washed flags, choose the sizes you want and use the stones whole.

Paving is for Large Areas

Stepping stones are the best answer for a path in a garden of modest size. They are more in scale, they look natural, they are relatively easy to install.

A large garden usually needs a bolder path than that provided by stepping stones, though they may be used to form secondary walks or side branches from a main path. A paved path is made up of a number of flat stones set close together to cover a sizeable area. If you need a path any wider than about 3 feet, paving is recommended.

The term "paving," as used in this book, does

not refer to masses of rolled asphalt or troweled concrete. There are several materials that can be arranged as paving that do not look like a portion of a freeway. Paving can be used for wide paths as well as for terrace or patio areas adjoining the house. The proper selection of materials will go a long way toward maintaining the natural appearance and blending house and garden.

■ *Brick*, when set in patterns such as herring bone or basket weave, is usually too formal for a path in a Japanese garden. Also, a large area would require such a number of bricks that almost any pattern would be too busy. Clinker brick does have surface patches and irregularities that make it look more unfinished and rustic than other varieties.

■ *Adobe block* can give an interesting combination of East and West in a Japanese garden. It has a warm, earthy feeling, owing to its brown color, rough surface, and uneven shape. Adobe block can be used all by itself to form a handsome paving or it can be combined with natural stone.

Though individual blocks are considerably larger than brick (they measure about 4 by 8 by 16 inches), they are too small for stepping stones. However, you can group two or three adobe blocks close together to form a stepping stone. Be sure to set at least a third of their depth in the ground.

■ *Tile* is much too formal and dressy for use in a Japanese garden, though in earthy colors it can be used effectively in a terrace or entry to connect house and garden.

■ *Cast concrete* does not have the natural appearance of stone, but it can be combined with stone to form a pleasing path, either as stepping stones or as paving. You can cast square or rectangular concrete stepping stones by building a form with 2 x 4's. Nail two corners, hinge the third, and put a hook on the fourth. Place the form over building paper, oil the form, and pour in concrete mixed in a ratio of 1:2:3 (cement: sand:gravel). When the concrete sets, remove the form, clean and re-oil it, and refill. While the

ROUGH, IRREGULAR *stones at left look an integral part of earth in which they rest. On right,* natural and cut stones *are laid on gravel; single rounded stone marks path intersection.*

concrete is still soft you can set cobbles into the surface, or "seed" the top with small gravel. Or, once it sets up, gently hose the surface to expose the aggregate.

For round or irregularly shaped stepping stones, curve a 2-inch strip of flat sheet metal into the form you wish on a bed of sand. Secure the ends of the form with a cotter pin or clamp, stake the outside for extra support, and oil the inside to prevent sticking.

Instead of casting concrete stepping stones and waiting until they are thoroughly cured to move them into their final position, you can pour each one in place. Lay out your path, establishing the location for each stone. Put the form where the stone is to remain and cast the stone directly on the soil. This assures that every stone will be perfectly fitted to the ground beneath and you won't have to level each one in place. To speed things up, make several forms so you can cast more than one stone at a time.

The simplest method of all for making concrete stepping stones is to pour them directly into an earth mold right where you want them. The earth-mold method works well for a paved path. Lay out the entire path, locating the position of each stone. Dig out the desired contour for each to a depth of 4 inches. Pour concrete and finish the surface in whatever way you wish. The mix shouldn't be too soupy so you can pour and trowel the stepping stones to bring the surface slightly higher than ground level.

If you don't cast in place, each block must be settled carefully so it rests solidly on the ground. If any block is unstable, it may crack over a long period of use.

Once concrete stepping stones or paving is cured (24 to 48 hours), fill in the spaces between with a rich soil mix.

PATHS THAT AREN'T STONE

Although stone paths are the best answer in most situations, there are some instances when you might better choose some other kind of path. In planning a path you should ask yourself how

 How to Construct a Stone Path

When you have a general idea of where you'd like a path, lay out its rough form with a length of rope or the garden hose. If you plan paving, use a pair of ropes parallel to each other to establish the sides.

If the path is to be made up of stepping stones, lay out a rough newspaper pattern, using a piece of paper for each stone. This will help you in locating the stones so they'll be easy to walk on and will give you a general idea of how much material you'll need.

Always place the primary—or largest—stones first, then work in the secondary, smaller ones. If you're working with a sand or soil base, or setting stones individually in concrete, you can locate all of the primary stones for the entire path then go back and work in the smaller ones. If you lay a paved path entirely on a concrete base, pour a few feet of concrete, set primary then secondary stones, pour more concrete, set more stones, and so on. Don't pour too far ahead of yourself or the concrete may start setting up while you're still fussing with the stones.

A paved path can be built on top of the existing grade, in which case you build a form with lumber and set the paving in a bed of concrete. Or, you can construct the paving to be just a little higher than grade by digging a trench which acts as a form for concrete (or for a sand base). In either case the soil should be compacted and watered before you pour. Lay fencing wire (2- to 4-inch mesh) in the form for reinforcing, pour the concrete, and set the stones.

Unless the base is solid concrete, fill in spaces between stones with good soil and wet the path with a fine spray of water. Add more soil if the first layer has settled, and plant ground cover to grow between stones.

Stones should be slightly higher than ground level to prevent soil from working over them or ground cover from growing completely over them.

As a final touch, you can edge a path with rocks, open fencing, wickets (made by forming hoops with strips of bamboo), or short lengths of unpeeled logs (redwood, cypress, cedar) 2 to 4 inches in diameter.

ROCK GARDEN with Japanese overtones was built where elbows of natural rock broke through soil. Broad concrete steps weave between stone outcroppings, looking almost like a stream.

stone will serve your own particular needs. Will stone work with any type of landscaping? Not always. If you have an existing terrace or patio set with tile, for example, you might better carry the feeling of the tile a little way into the garden rather than create an abrupt transition by switching to a totally different material.

If you are building a Japanese garden from scratch, you're probably safe in planning stone paths since you can landscape the entire garden with that in mind. But if you're adding a garden or modifying one to go with an established scheme, choose path materials and a design that will work harmoniously with what you have.

The advantages of stone paths usually outweigh any disadvantages. Nevertheless, you should be aware of several good and bad points. On the good side, stone is durable, probably longer-lasting than any other material. If a portion of a stone path should become damaged, it can easily be repaired. The stone itself almost never needs replacing or renewing. Of all materials, stone is perhaps the best for achieving the natural look so essential in a Japanese garden. Stone paths blend best with most other elements in the garden—rock arrangements, lanterns, plantings, structures.

On the other hand, a stone path can be a difficult surface for older people as well as toddlers. Though not prohibitively expensive, the cost of installing stone may be more than, say, swept earth (but less than gravel). Dirt and dust tend to collect on paving, and leaves and weeds can add to your maintenance of stepping stones.

If stone isn't for you, you might consider bare earth, gravel, wood chips, or wooden rounds.

ENTRY AND SIDE GARDENS are divided by pass-through flanked by large piece of driftwood and light bamboo sleeve fence. The gravel is punctuated by redwood rounds. (Design, Kaye Scott.)

Earth is the Most Simple Path

The most natural path of all is one worn by constant traffic, one with no artificial bounds. Since it's unlikely that you'll have enough traffic to keep a path beaten, and since nature has a way of claiming soil that isn't controlled by the hand of man, you'll have to add a minimum of effort to keep an earth path usable.

An earth path is simple, as is its construction. First of all, soak the earth thoroughly with a sprinkler or by flooding until you've softened the top 3 or 4 inches of soil. Next, use a hoe to strip at least 2 inches off the top, removing weeds, grasses, and their roots. Cut a path between 2 feet and 4 feet wide. Remove any rocks or other rubble that does not lie flat with the stripped surface, and use hoe and rake to get the path fairly smooth. It's best to have the path slightly higher in the center than at the edges, to keep water from puddling where you walk.

Now use a roller or tamper to compact the soil. Water the path and compact it two or three times, raking off any pebbles that are not pressed down.

That's all there is to it. To keep weeds down, you'll have to spray the path occasionally, being very careful that the spray doesn't get to neighboring plantings. If the path gets dusty, sprinkle it with water; if it gets rough, sprinkle and roll it.

RAISED WOODEN walkway is bold path through restful entry garden. Pool backed by Japanese maple; left of lantern is Colorado spruce. Notice excellent use of borrowed scenery. (Design, George Murata.)

SMOOTH, BLACK STONES are set into staggered concrete pads edged with redwood headers. Tall plantings of timber bamboo, camellia, mahonia repeat lines of gate and direct the eye along path.

The Sound of Gravel Underfoot

Gravel and crushed rock enjoy several advantages over other surfacing materials for paths. A gravel path dries quickly. Dirt spilled on gravel can easily be washed away. Neither rain nor a hosing will leave standing puddles.

Gravel can be a slow and uncomfortable surface; little stones find their way into shoes or get kicked out alongside the path. It gradually works into the soil beneath and must be replenished from time to time. And, you just can't rake leaves easily out of gravel.

Gravel stands up best if you put it down as a topping over a more permanent bed of redrock or decomposed granite. Heavy-grade polyethylene sheeting or tarpaper is an effective bedding for a gravel walk; it holds down weeds as well as holding up the gravel. Perforate either, about one hole per square foot, to let water drain away. If you don't use sheeting, control weed growth by spraying.

A gravel path should have header boards to contain the small stones and to help keep ground

cover from growing into the path. After grading the area for the path, dig 2-inch trenches along both sides and lay in redwood 2 x 4's on edge. Use 18-inch stakes alternating on either side at close intervals; drive the tops of the stakes below the top of the headers so soil will conceal them on one side and gravel on the other. Ground covers alongside the path will soon cover the headers.

For best results, gravel should be rolled. Rake it over the area in thin layers, dampen it, and roll it. Repeat until the area is built up to the final thickness.

The average pebble side should be about $\frac{1}{2}$ inch. Anything smaller will be kicked around too much; anything larger is too difficult to walk on. For 100 square feet of 2-inch-deep surfacing you'll need $\frac{2}{3}$ cubic yard of gravel.

Crushed rock makes a presentable path as long as you stay away from artificially colored materials or dolomite (which is glaring white). Crushed rock packs down tight and stays in place.

You can make a handsome path by combining gravel and stepping stones. Prepare the area as you would for a gravel path, only set the stepping stones firmly in place before adding the gravel.

Since the stones will carry most of the traffic, the gravel needn't be compacted as much as a regular gravel path. Also, to give the path a more open feeling, you can omit header boards and let the gravel mingle with ground cover along the edges. You will have to keep close control on the ground cover so it doesn't take over the entire path.

Gravel by itself may slow you down when you walk on it, but who wants to hurry through the garden? And there's nothing quite like the sound of gravel underfoot.

How About Wood Chips?

Wood chips, firbark, and other similar wood products make soft, springy paths that look and feel natural. Usually they are too lightweight for full foot traffic—they get kicked all over the place—and are best used in combination with stepping stones. Fine-ground bark and sawdust are too fine for use as a path.

Firbark and wood chips are susceptible to bacteria or insect infestation unless properly drained. To carry water off, pitch a path slightly toward an area with good drainage. To discourage insects, spray on a commercial wood preservative while raking the material several times. Soil beneath a wood path should be sterilized to minimize weed growth, but fallen leaves can be left to disintegrate into the wood.

A ton of firbark (approximately 3 to 4 cubic yards) will cover about 200 square feet to a depth of 2 inches. It is usually available from garden and building material suppliers in the following sizes (particle diameter): $^1/_8$ to $^3/_4$ inch; 1 inch; $1^1/_2$ to $2^1/_2$ inches.

Wooden Rounds for a Rustic Touch

Round discs cut straight through the trunk of a redwood, cedar, or cypress tree can be put down in sand as individual stepping stones, or they can be set close together to form a paved path.

Wooden rounds, or blocks, are not permanent. At best they'll give perhaps 10 or 15 years of service; under unfavorable conditions you may have to replace them in two or three years. Generally, the drier they are the longer they'll last. However, in sunny, hot locations rounds will crack and warp. In heavy frosts they will freeze and split.

A thorough application of a toxic wood preservative should lengthen the lifespan of wooden stepping stones or paving by several years. A 5% solution of pentachlorophenol gives good protection, but since it's toxic to plant life it may discourage any plantings you might want to grow between rounds. Copper naphthenate is an excellent preservative but it imparts a green tint to the wood. (The color will eventually weather to a dark brown; to avoid it altogether, treat only the bottoms of the rounds.) Be sure to use a type of preservative that has a toxic agent included in the formula to help protect against insect invasion. Theoretically termites do not bother redwood; actually they'll attack it if it's around long enough. Remember that any preservative must soak well into the wood to do its job; merely brushing on a coat that stains the surface is not enough protection.

End-grain blocks cut from railroad ties tend to last a fairly long time because they have at one time been pressure-treated with creosote. Cut to

 Basic Materials for Garden Paths

Everyone has his own reason for liking, or not liking, certain materials for a garden path. Each material has characteristics that make it ideal in one situation, objectionable in another. Here are some of the most commonly used path materials for a Japanese garden, along with a brief summary of their advantages and shortcomings.

■ *Earth.* The simplest of paths, and perhaps the most rustic of all. If the soil is well compacted, dust is negligible, but rains can turn even the best of earth paths into slippery, sticky mud.

■ *Gravel.* Comparatively inexpensive, simple to install, easy to maintain (just add fresh gravel). If the pebbles are too small, they'll be kicked out of place; if too large, they're uncomfortable underfoot. Keeping gravel free of leaves can be a chore.

■ *Stone.* Flags, bricks, concrete, or adobe blocks laid either as paving or stepping stones are long-lived. Installation can be tricky, depending on the path configuration. In damp or shady areas the path may get mossy and slippery.

■ *Wood.* Easy to put in, wood chips or sawdust are also easily kicked or blown out of place. Wooden rounds are more stable and fairly permanent.

CUT STONE BLOCKS almost as thick as they are wide make level path across pond. At right, path made from old Hawaiian millstones, granite slabs (Design, C. J. & R. O. Thompson).

. . . WOODEN ROUNDS

a length of 6 to 8 inches, they are best set close together and used as paving. To set blocks in place, excavate an area to a depth 1 inch greater than the thickness of the blocks. Use 1 x 4 inch redwood headers, burying half of their width below grade. Tamp the ground and cover it with 1 inch of sand, then place the blocks level with the edging, separated from each other by about 1 inch. Adjust their spacing until they fill the area to be covered, then pour or sweep sand down the joints.

To set rounds, grade the soil as above but omit header boards; the large discs are less likely to move around than the smaller blocks. Put down a 2-inch bed of sand, place the rounds on it, using large ones for major steps and smaller ones in between to fill out the design of the path. Fill in with soil that will support moss, wet the path down, and add more soil if needed.

Flat stones look best sitting somewhat higher than the surrounding surface, but wooden rounds appear best when they are almost flush with grade. In shady locations moss will usually grow around the edges of rounds. If moss begins to take over the surface, making it slippery in wet weather, just scrape it off or sprinkle sand on top.

STEPS TO GO UP OR DOWN

A change in level within the garden adds a point of special interest. Even if it isn't necessary to go up a hill or descend into a hollow, a couple of steps that make a path go up or down can offset what might otherwise be a monotonous flatness.

Almost any garden of any size has space for a few steps. Create a hillock by mounding up earth, or make a slight depression by scooping out a hollow. Be sure to plan either one so it will be integrated with the rest of the garden. A mound that sticks up in the middle of a pancake-level area for no apparent reason can look very artificial. A streambed is a fairly good reason to work in some high and low spots in the garden.

Steps usually don't exist by themselves but are an extension of a path. Thus, you will usually want to construct steps using the same materials used in the path. Combine steps and a path harmoniously. A path should leisurely lead into steps, not terminate abruptly in a sharp stairway whose steepness tires you out just looking at it.

Like a path, steps can be made from earth, wood, stone, or combination of several materials. For a formal arrangement use pre-cast concrete blocks, or cut-stone blocks, overlapping one on the other slightly at each step. Wide, flat flag-

REDWOOD ROUNDS are the only decorative pieces in gravelled entry (Design, George Hay). At right, an arched slab of cut granite bridges stream inlet to pond (Design, George Kubota).

stones can be set into earth, resting on one another (overlapping), or each step can be spaced a couple of feet back from the previous one with soil packed between to make a deep tread.

Usually a few large stones will make a handsome series of steps from the garden to floor level of the house, or up to a deck or engawa. One large flat rock can be used as the traditional shoe-removing stone—see the photo on page 6.

For a rustic appearance set logs, wooden rounds, or railroad ties either as tight steps or steps with earth treads—see the drawings on page 108. You can use gravel or firbark to fill in between the wooden risers, but you'll have to replenish it occasionally.

Garden steps should be wide with low risers, since they are an extension of a path designed for strolling rather than for busy traffic. They should look comfortable and be comfortable. They don't have to go straight up. After working out the best combination that fits the change in levels, fit it to the slope by breaking the distance with landings, curve the steps, or zig-zag them.

Figure on 2 to 5 feet for step width in the garden. With stepping stones the individual stones can be smaller as long as the overall width is not less than 2 feet. Risers (the vertical part of a step) should not be higher than about 8 inches; treads (the horizontal part) should be no less than 12 inches deep.

Steps must be firmly located so they won't rock or tip underfoot. Don't just set flagstones or wooden rounds on top of the soil but settle them well into the earth so they can't work loose.

Even for a flight of several steps in the garden, an informal arrangement doesn't require the kind of foundation that would be needed for formal stairs. If over a year or two portions of steps settle or tip, this adds to their rustic feeling, as long as the steps remain solid enough to walk on. Unless you must have a long flight of stairs, you probably won't need a concrete foundation but can set steps in sand, gravel, crushed rock, or directly into the earth.

For a long slope where the pitch is not great enough for a flight of steps but is too great for a path, consider ramp steps. For risers, use whole logs, split logs, fence posts, railroad ties, or large stone flags (any wood that touches soil should be treated with preservative). Fill the space between risers to a depth of 3 to 5 inches with gravel, firbark, or compacted earth. For comfortable use, the ramp between risers should be about 4 or 5 feet deep, and the ramps should not rise any more than about 3 inches from front to back.

Keep plantings around steps under control. Ground covers that grow close to the edges of steps help to blend them with the rest of the garden but ivy that is allowed to spread over steps can be hazardous.

USE A BRIDGE FOR BRIDGING

Most gardens have no need for a footbridge. A bridge should be used to cross a pond or stream —either dry or with water—that is too wide to cross with one or two stepping stones. A bridge should be functional—it need not be large but it should be sturdy enough to be walked on. Too often a homeowner will install a quaint wooden arch in the garden that bridges nothing and goes nowhere. Such a structure used in this manner adds next to nothing to the garden and actually detracts from it by calling attention to its own incongruous cuteness.

The simplest way of crossing a small stream is to carry the line of a path across with large stepping stones set in the water. This is not really a bridge but an extension of a path.

A small rustic bridge can be made by merely laying a sturdy plank from bank to bank. For interest, use two planks of the same length side by side but offset them several inches so their ends are staggered. Use 2 x 10 unfinished redwood, with a couple of 1 x 4 inch battens nailed across the underside to hold the planks together.

The same type of bridge can be made using one or two slabs of cut stone.

You can cast a slab bridge in reinforced concrete right on the spot. Pour into a pre-built form in place, and when the concrete has set remove the sides of the form but leave the bottom—it'll never be seen.

Some garden supply centers or specialty stone yards may have curved granite slabs that will give an arch to a stone bridge. Since these are imported from Japan, they are much more expensive than either a plank bridge or one you cast yourself.

For spanning a distance of any more than 4 or 5 feet, a bridge structure should be supported by a foundation, by stone banks, or by mid-span piers and trestles. A foundation can be merely two blocks of concrete, one at each end, poured directly into holes dug in the ground. Set a couple of reinforcing rods vertically into each foundation when you pour, letting them extend far enough out that you can secure the bridge structure to them. When the bridge is in place, conceal the foundation with soil, rocks, and plantings.

Piers can be made from pressure-treated poles sunk into the bottom of a pond or wide stream to

---

 Four Types of Garden Steps

Shown below are construction tips on three types of wooden steps and one of stone. Redwood rounds, obtainable at most lumber yards, may split when dry, so settle them firmly in the soil. Make log risers by splitting or sawing 2-foot to 4-foot lengths, or use pre-split firewood. For railroad ties,

watch for newspaper advertisements or ads in home magazines, or check with lumber yards.

Railroad ties are treated to resist decay; any wood that rests on soil should be.

When ordering stone for steps, choose rocks for steps yourself to make sure surfaces are flat.

REDWOOD rounds should be offset from side to side for interest.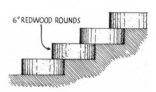

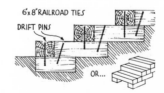 *RAILROAD ties make a formal but long-lived set of garden steps.*

WHOLE or half logs need to be anchored well with stakes or pipes.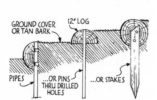

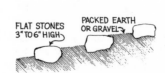 *FLAT stones can be separated, as shown, or overlap each other.*

GARDEN STEPS at top are packed earth, with rock and split stake risers. Lower steps are cut stone in bed of fir bark. Wooden bridge at right is yatsuhashi type (see the text below).

give center support to a bridge. Simpler yet, support the center of a low bridge on a large rock.

Arrange rocks both on the banks and in the water beneath the end of a bridge. This will give the feeling of a more intimate contact between the bridge and the water. Flat, unarched bridges should be from 6 inches to a foot above the surface of the water (or the simulated surface of a dry stream). If the distance is much more than that the feeling of intimacy may be lost.

There is a wooden zig-zag bridge, called *yatsu-hashi*, commonly used in Japanese gardens. It is fairly easy to construct since it is quite rustic, but it shouldn't be used unless you have a sizeable pond to cross. Use pairs of planks, or split logs with their flat surface up, laid side by side on short wooden piles. Zig-zag each pair in order that the total length of the bridge is much more than would be that of a straight span. In Japan this kind of bridge is often used to cross above beds of water plants. The indirect route induces one to linger long enough to enjoy the flowers or watch the fish in the water below.

Another kind of plank bridge on pilings uses two or three lengths laid side by side then continued by another group laid in the same direction but with their ends staggered or offset from the ends of the first group. As many of these off-set groups are used as needed to cross a body of water. Instead of crossing in a straight line you walk the length of one set of planks, then make a turn and another turn to proceed.

The reason for such an interesting configuration has its roots in Japanese folklore: If someone were pursued by the Devil, he could run across the bridge and make the sudden turn to right or left. The Devil, being unaware of the scheme, would race straight ahead and so charge off the bridge to drown in the water.

A simple bridge can be made by laying two wide logs or half-logs from bank to bank, spacing them 2 to 3 feet apart, then nailing small branches (about 3 inches in diameter) close together across the logs. The earth bridge (*dobashi*) is an elaboration on this basic scheme. After the crosspieces are secured, bundles of tied rushes are fastened along the edges as a sort of curbing. Then a mixture of earth and gravel is packed down between the edgings.

The photo on page 4 shows a variation on this scheme. The framework or base of the high-arch bridge illustrated is reinforced concrete. The edges of the lower portion of the bridge look like natural logs but actually are concrete. On top are straight lengths of tree limbs 2 to 3 inches in diameter, edged with a curbing of tied rushes.

GARDEN GATES play a double role: When closed they should be imposing enough to imply privacy; when open they should be inviting and entice you to visit garden. (Design, George Kubota.)

Ways to Enclose Your Garden

Landscaping with fences.....closed fences for privacy...open fences for special effects...stone walls...hedges...gates

Fences, walls, hedges—all are means for enclosing an area, for separating one area from another. But a fence can perform other functions as well as enclosing and separating. It can help to visually contain a property; it can architecturally tie house and garden together; it can modify structural lines of buildings and blend them with landscaping; it can add an intimate, cozy feeling; it can provide privacy and even weather control.

The Japanese garden usually identifies with two general types of enclosures: one that forms a boundary and sets off the garden from the rest of the neighborhood; and one that separates areas within the garden. Either type can be a fence, constructed of wood or some other natural material; either can be hedge, created by living plants; either can be a wall, made of stone or earth.

It's clear that there is a wide variety of forms and materials that will do the utilitarian job, first,

of enclosing, and, second, of establishing a definite mood or feeling. Rather than impulsively throwing up a slat fence just because it costs less than another kind, you should spend some time and thought trying to choose the right kind of enclosure for your particular situation, and thus to some measure assure that you are going to be reasonably pleased with it when you have it. A shrub can usually be dug up and transferred to another location, and a stone lantern can be moved out of a garden entirely, but a fence or hedge represents a fairly permanent installation and should be planned carefully before being committed.

Here are a few guides to help you in thinking about enclosures. Read and remember them before driving a single nail or piling up two rocks.

■ *Need.* Does your garden really need a fence? Will a fence serve a purpose—even if only an esthetic one? Not every Japanese garden needs

to be closed off completely, and not every garden must have dividing fences within it.

■ *Purpose.* If you feel that your garden will benefit by an enclosure, determine its purpose. Is it to provide privacy, to blend house and garden, to soften architectural lines, to separate one area from another, to strengthen the Oriental feeling? Only after deciding what you want an enclosure to do should you start thinking about what you want it to look like.

■ *Appearance.* The appearance of an enclosure should answer its purpose as well as your personal tastes. A fence intended to surround a garden and give it complete privacy should be high and it should be closed construction. On the other hand, a fence intended to visually separate a pond from a walk need be only a couple of feet high and might be open bamboo grillwork. The appearance of an enclosure will depend also on the feeling it is to convey: A massive stone wall says "Keep Out!" A low hedge stops traffic but

SIDE VIEW OF GATE, and accompanying fence shown on previous page. Fence roof is shingled to complement feeling of gate roof. Driftwood, bamboo are used in fence "peek through" sections.

... FENCING GUIDES

invites you to stroll. The appearance of a fence, or hedge, will be influenced to a very great degree by the style of the garden and the architecture of the house. As a general rule, the simpler the garden the simpler should be its enclosures. An ornately carved fence and gate would overpower a small Zen garden, and a rustic rail fence would be out of place with a very formal style of garden.
■ *Cost.* Though not first on the list, cost is also not last. If you expect an enclosure to enhance your garden, let cost be a governing factor but not a controlling one. If you are going to do the work yourself, discuss your ideas with a lumber dealer, nurseryman, or garden equipment supplier. They

are familiar with materials, their uses, and their costs. They can help you develop your ideas as well as suggest ways to keep things within a budget. If you plan to have a professional do the job, have a clear understanding of his fees and methods and feel free—before the work begins—to talk over alternative approaches in order that you can weigh styles of enclosures and materials to best give you what you can afford and will also be happy with.
■ *Legal Aspects.* Somewhere along the line of your planning, before your mind is really set on a fence of a certain height and style, be sure to check local ordinances. Some municipalities require a building permit for a fence. Local ordinances may restrict the height of boundary fences to 3 or 4 feet. Most cities also specify how close

to a sidewalk or street you can build a fence. Some cities even specify the kinds of materials that can be used. Restrictions and ordinances are for your protection as well as your neighbor's, so be sure to work within them. Give your City Hall or County Courthouse a call.

■ *Neighbors.* If the planned fence will be inside your property line, you have little to worry about in regard to neighbors. If a fence is to straddle a boundary line, you and your neighbor will have to reach an agreement on its style and appearance since he has to look at it too. Even though it's pretty much your own business what you do on your own property, when you plan something massive in a close neighborhood it's a good idea to at least drop a hint to your neighbor as to what's happening.

LANDSCAPING WITH FENCES

Enclosing a garden gives a certain feeling of coziness. A fence can transform a big, open lot into a quiet, enclosed area. And, if you confine your Japanese landscaping to only a portion of your property, a properly designed fence can serve the dual purpose of separating the areas yet blending them so that neither one seems totally divorced from the other.

Avoid having a fence look as if it's standing all by itself. Soften its lines by bringing rocks and plantings up to the structure. Very large rocks can be made part of a fence by building it right over them, fitting boards to the rock's contours. Smaller rocks can be used in arrangements close

BOARD FENCE made by alternating planks on either side of rails acts as wind baffle, has interesting shadow patterns that repeat vertical lines of gate. Rough-sawn wood scorched with torch.

FENCE WITH SECTIONS of board and sections of bamboo has an interesting variety. Rocks and shrubs close to fence blend its height with rest of the landscaping. (Design, George Kubota.)

. . . LANDSCAPING FENCES

to a fence or even laid out along the base to serve as a visual foundation.

A stone lantern can often be displayed to an advantage against a fence. If lighted at night, it will cast interesting shadow patterns.

You can also utilize winter shadows cast by deciduous trees planted near a fence. Ginkgo, sweet gum, horsechestnut, dogwood, Chinese pistache, maples, and most of the flowering fruit trees have distinctive forms that add visual value to the garden when silhouetted against a plain background. Trees and shrubs with showy fruits and berries or with dramatic leaves often display well against a fence. Tall-growing bamboo is effective if it's kept pruned high so the stems can be seen.

One of the best ways to blend a fence with the garden is to train vines to grow on it. Keep the vines under control, however, so the entire fence won't lose its structural individuality by being buried under a mass of foliage. The following are but a few vines that can be grown effectively on

or against a fence; see your nursery for others: clematis, wisteria, Virginia creeper, small-leafed ivy, bougainvillea, fatshedera, star jasmine.

Fences or walls are strong architectural elements. Especially in a small garden, open space is important to avoid a sense of being crowded and closed in. A feeling of coziness is one thing; a feeling of confinement is something else. Use enclosures where they will serve a purpose but don't allow them to get out of hand and partition an otherwise uncrowded area into cubicles.

CLOSED OR OPEN FENCE?

A closed fence is one that offers a solid barrier, whatever its height. Closed fences are more often used as boundary fences around a Japanese garden rather than as enclosures within the garden, since their main purpose is to provide privacy and establish a definite isolation. In windy areas closed fences should be of sturdy construction. A closed fence will block wind, but often will act as a baffle and roll strong wind right into the garden. A closed fence creates its own microclimates: the sunny side will reflect heat, and the shady side will have cooler pockets, so plan your plantings accordingly.

Some examples of closed fence construction are tight-set board, board and batten, tight-set slat or stake, tight-woven wood, bamboo, or reed.

An open fence affords less privacy than a closed one, since its construction is basically that of spaced-out boards or slats or an open grillwork. But a tall enclosure that completely surrounds a garden has a lighter feeling if it is open.

An open fence will usually break up wind flow, often providing better wind protection than a closed one. An open fence can be less expensive to build, since generally it has less material in it than a solid fence.

Open fences can be used effectively as complete enclosures for small lots, as in many suburban developments or metropolitan areas. Open construction is most often used for small fences within the garden.

Some examples of open construction are widely spaced slats, stakes, or boards; louvered boards; board-and-board; lattice; rail.

You can often combine closed and open construction in a single fence. Though the aim of a closed fence is privacy, some open grillwork at the top gives it a freer feeling. In Japan it is common to find fences or even walls that are solid from the ground up to about eye-level, where there is a "peek-through" section of lattice that softens the line of the enclosure.

Small Fences within the Garden

The *sode-gaki* is a small fence usually used within the garden to divide or separate areas rather than close them off completely. The name means "sleeve fence," owing to the fence's resemblance to the long sleeve of a kimono. This type of screen fence is fast becoming popular in many Western gardens even where no attempt is made to maintain a Japanese theme. Strategically placed sleeve fences can create interesting areas within the garden. They can conceal a service yard, wood pile, dog run, garbage can, or hose storage. They can provide a backdrop for a bonsai display or a special rock grouping.

Sleeve fences usually abut the house and thus help to connect house and garden. However, one end of a sleeve fence can connect with a boundary fence or a garden structure such as a tea house. Or, it can stand alone. A freestanding sleeve fence should be blended into the garden with plantings or rocks.

 How to Use a Standard Fence Frame

Board fences are simple to construct, and the proper configuration can carry through the theme of naturalness necessary to a Japanese garden. Shown below are several variations on filling in a standard wood frame.

Dimensions are fairly standardized. Favored heights are 5 feet 6 inches or 6 feet. Posts are 6 by 6's or 4 by 4's, set 6 to 8 feet apart. Standard 2 by 4's serve as top and bottom rails.

Either rough or finished lumber can be used for framing and for filling in. Redwood is good for framing, since it resists decay. Posts should be set in concrete 1½ feet deep, with a concrete cap several inches above soil level sloped away from the post. As additional protection treat post bottoms with preservative solutions before setting them in the ground.

Leave the wood unfinished to weather naturally.

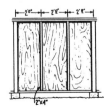

VARIETY OF FENCES based on standard frame. Left to right: vertical slats, open top and bottom; wide plank, 2 by 4 "batts"; alternating planks; horizontal slats; reed or bamboo, with open section.

Keep these small fences in scale with the rest of the surroundings and repeat materials used elsewhere in the garden. A height of 2 to 5 feet is a good average, and a length of 3 to 8 feet will still keep the fence within the realm of a sode-gaki; anything much bigger becomes a full-fledged enclosure.

Sode-gaki can be of closed or open construction. They can be formed from a single straight section, or one section can meet another to make a corner. At its simplest, a sleeve fence can be an open lattice of bamboo lashed or wired together; or it can be a section of board fencing complete with thatched roof. In Japan sleeve fences are made from cylindrical bundles of rushes, of woven reed, or of tied twigs. Since there is virtually no limit to the number of possible designs,

the sleeve fence is as much a test of the owner's ingenuity as is a garden gate.

Some garden supply specialists sell handsome sode-gaki made in Japan. Since a sleeve fence is a comparatively simple structure, you might enjoy building your own, using materials available in your area.

Some Construction Pointers

In the true Japanese garden natural materials are preferred for fences and gates. Iron or wire fences are seldom used except to enclose large properties, and even then they are not considered a part of the garden. Wood is the favored material, because of its strength and natural appearance.

Wood should not be painted but should be allowed to weather naturally (redwood will eventually turn almost black; pine and fir become a dull gray; cedar weathers to a silvery gray). You

PERHAPS THE MOST SIMPLE fence of all is formed by bending strips of bamboo croquet-wicket fashion, forcing ends into ground. Fence is inexpensive, fragile, but directs garden traffic.

FENCES AT LEFT are at opposite ends of formality scale; top one needs repairing occasionally as posts deteriorate. Photo at right shows details of tied bamboo. (Design, Shinichi Maesaki).

can stain a fence, or simulate age and weathering by sandblasting, wire brushing, or scorching the surface with a flame from a gas torch. If you're lucky, you might manage to fall heir to naturally weathered siding from a demolished barn; it can make a fine looking fence.

You can construct almost any style board fence using a standard frame—see page 115. Use 2 x 4 lumber for upper and lower rails, and 4 x 4 posts. Fill in the frame with board and board, board and batten, close-set or spaced out stakes or slats, or louvers, any of which can be in either a horizontal or vertical arrangement. Or, with the basic frame, use bamboo, reed, or basket weave in either a closed or open lattice design.

The most permanent fence is constructed around posts set in concrete. Redwood posts that have been chemically treated can be set directly into the ground as long as the soil is tamped well around them a little at a time. They won't be quite as sturdy or long-lasting as posts set in concrete but if the rest of the fence is properly built, they'll probably last five to ten years.

Sleeve fences can usually be constructed around posts or vertical supports driven or set into the ground. Since they aren't intended to do a major job of screening, and since they are comparatively small, repairing or replacing them isn't the major job it can be with a complete boundary fence.

With any fence, construct it to last as long as possible. A fence can look delicate and light, but it should not be so flimsy that an enthusiastic dog could knock it flat.

Bamboo or reed fencing is relatively short-lived but the low cost and ease of replacement

STURDY BUTTRESSES projecting at right angles to gate and fence add some physical support but are used mainly to visually stabilize mass of gate and help break straight line of fence.

. . . SLEEVE FENCES

makes it worthwhile, even if it has to be replaced after three or four years. You can extend the life of either bamboo or reed by giving it a couple of coats of flat-finish, clear sealer.

The small roof you see running along some of the fences shown in this book is more than decorative. It also serves the very practical purpose of keeping rain off the top of the fence, thus prolonging its life. If your house roof is shingled, using the same materials for a fence roof will help to blend the architecture into the garden.

Fences You Tie Together

Bamboo is one of the oldest and most common fencing materials in a Japanese garden. It's easy to handle and it has an Oriental feeling that no other material can claim. Some lumberyards, garden suppliers, or sporting goods stores stock "fishing pole" bamboo, averaging 1 inch in diameter and running to a length of 10 to 15 feet, which is ideal for tied sleeve fences.

Lash horizontal and vertical members together with wire (twist the ends and bend them down after cutting them short, to prevent things being snagged or scratched). Or use heavy twine (but not plastic clothesline) that has been dyed by being dipped in stain or creosote. Tie a square knot and let the ends extend an inch or so.

For posts, use large timber bamboo or several small stems tied together. Better yet, use redwood posts and lash a bamboo lattice to them, up off the ground.

Cut the tops of vertical pieces of bamboo just above a joint to prevent rain and dirt from collecting inside.

Tied fences should be used chiefly within the garden. Though bamboo is used most often, you can make a tied fence using split stakes or slats for a horizontal or vertical lattice.

STONE WALLS AND HEDGES

Walls and hedges are occasionally used as boundary enclosures in Japan, some being as much as 10 feet high. Solid walls are constructed of field stone, often of plastered mud or clay mixed with straw or fragments of old roof tiles. Plaster walls

Nine Useful Garden Gates

| ROOFED GATES | BOUNDARY GATES | INNER GATES |

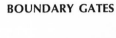

SHAPED-BOARD RIDGEPOLE　　*PLANK-BAMBOO GATE*　　*CURVED LOG CROSSPIECE*

TIED BAMBOO ROOF　　*FORMAL GATE, POSTS*　　*ROUGH LOG POSTS*

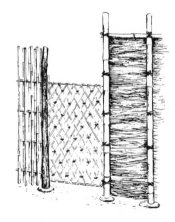

SHINGLED ROOF　　*DIAGONAL LATTICE GATE*　　*"LIFTING" LATTICE GATE*

TIGHTLY WOVEN MATTING, vertical reed, tied bamboo are combined in gate at left. Gate at right has tied reed, ornately carved crosspiece, and carved panels. (Design, Shinichi Maesaki.)

. . . WALLS

are capped with a small wooden or tile roof to keep rain from disintegrating the materials. They are left in their natural earthy color or else are whitewashed.

The result is a formidable barrier, but one that fits in with both old and contemporary architecture. As formal as a plastered wall might seem, the bits of tile or straw mixed in during construction give it a great deal of charm.

Not all homes look good with such a massive enclosure, and not all metropolitan areas have a building code that permits their construction. A large estate, a beach property, or a desert lot are sites where a high wall works well architecturally and does not overpower the surroundings by its sheer mass.

In certain areas of the United States walls are being used more and more. A substantial masonry wall will deaden sound; it provides a measure of privacy on both sides; it has insulating qualities; and there's nothing quite like a masonry wall for strength.

DELICATE FENCE and gate separate outer and inner gardens of classical tea garden. The small gate combines diagonal lattice with vertical lattice, separated by gnarled branch. (Design, Shinichi Maesaki.)

A wall—perhaps even more than a fence— should be in harmony with the house, since it is such a strong design element. A wall that is improperly blended will stand out like a sore thumb, so if you are thinking about a wall, be sure to consider all of the tips regarding fences given on page 111.

Natural stone for a wall should come from the site itself or from the immediate area. This works out well in the desert and at some sea-side locations where there is usually plenty of stone lying around. Being part of the natural landscape, it makes a wall "belong." If natural stone is hard to come by or too expensive, your only answer may be brick or concrete block.

Bricks and Blocks

Used brick does not represent much of a cost savings over new brick, but used in conjunction with a natural garden it has much more of a rustic feeling. Adobe block is substantial, and its earthy color and irregular texture have a natural warmth that fits in with almost any kind of landscaping. Concrete blocks will give you a sturdy wall, ideal in most respects, but unfortunately its appearance can be cold and artificial around a Japanese garden. The contemporary look of concrete block can be softened somewhat by constructing the wall in units between wood framing and letting the wood show. You can get the same effect by first building a solid wall, then adding a visual framing by attaching 2 x 4's or 1 x 2's directly to its surface to create a lattice effect with wood.

Shrubs and vines will also help to soften the lines of a concrete block wall. Leaving the mortar unraked, just as it squeezes out of the joints, will add a rustic touch.

It's common practice in Japan to build a low masonry wall—say, to a height of 2 or 3 feet—and construct a fence on it. A low wall can be topped with either a closed or open fence. Usually an open fence will offset the visual weight of the wall. If you try this scheme, build supports for the fence into the masonry. Set posts in concrete poured into the holes of concrete block, or set steel plates into the binding mortar to which you later bolt posts.

The proper choice of concrete block will go a long way toward making the difference between a stark, barren enclosure befitting a mausoleum, and an appealing, informal wall that looks as if it belongs with the garden. There is a wide selection of shapes and textures available. Some of the more decorative blocks (or even ordinary concrete blocks set on their sides so their holes show) can be used for constructing a grillwork wall. A masonry grille can be a strong visual element, so use plantings to keep it from dominating an area.

Dry Walls, Retaining Walls

A dry wall is a stone wall assembled without mortar. The stones are carefully fitted together so they hold each other in place by weight and friction. A dry wall requires some patience because you often have to lift several rocks into place to find one that makes a good fit.

A freestanding wall is built without a deep foundation, so its base stones should be larger than those in the wall. Bond stones, which pass entirely through the wall, hold the wall together. A gate post abutting a freestanding wall requires mortared joints, and the post should be set into the ground.

For a retaining wall place stones so the back ends tip down into the ground and the front faces, as seen in profile, slant upward. Set each course of stones back slightly from those beneath, so the entire wall leans into the hill. The steeper the bank, or the higher the wall, the steeper should be the slope to the wall.

Plant hedge or a row of bamboo along the top of a retaining wall to give it height, low shrubs for a subdued feeling.

Clipped hedges are used as complete enclosures for the garden and are also effective within the garden along a walk or as a screen. Clipped

 ## How to Choose and Use Gate Hardware

Gate hardware should be sturdy enough to hold up under constant use. Usually it's better to use hardware that is slightly oversized than that which is too small and will have to be replaced sooner than later.

Make sure that latch screws are long enough to go at least an inch into the timber. Latches take a real beating and screws will work loose quickly if they are too short. Most latches are made to be used with a padlock for complete closure. To secure a wooden sliding bolt, fasten a hasp to it on the inside of the gate and use either a lock or wooden pin.

The sturdiest hinges are those that have bolts which go deep into heavy timber or pass all the way through. Strap, butt, and "T" hinges will do the job if they are large enough and their screws are long enough. Before mounting any hinges be sure to decide whether you want the gate to swing in or out.

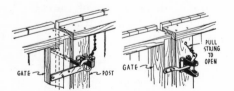

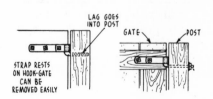

ONLY TWO of many types of gate latches are shown here; you can use a padlock with either for extra security. Wooden sliding bolt is home-made. Post-bolt hinges are strong, easy to install.

HOME-MADE gate latch at left was rough-cut from wood, then shaped with rasp and file (Design, Toshio Saburomaru). Heavy sliding bolt was made with 2 by 4, iron brackets.

hedges make good boundary fences, and informally trained hedges work well within the garden.

Boxwood, yew, privet, and arborvitae are but a few hardy shrubs that do well as clipped hedges. See your nurseryman for other plants suitable in your area and for advice on planting distance and care. Formal hedges need frequent clipping to keep their shape.

Informal hedges need only occasional trimming so they don't become too dense or overgrown. Close plantings of azalea or Japanese camellia make excellent informal hedges; other good candidates are Mexican orange, mirror plant, natal plum. One of the best of all hedge plants is bamboo. Depending on the type, you can have a hedge as high as 20 feet (really a living fence) or as low as 6 inches. See page 64 for tips on using bamboo.

A GATEWAY IS AN OPENING

The gateway is one of the most important features in a Japanese garden. No matter how simple and functional a boundary fence may be, a great deal of attention is given to the gateway to make it picturesque. Gateways inside the garden are fairly straightforward in keeping with the peaceful mood within, but the design and appearance of main gateways and gates are a work of art.

Nevertheless, gateways are never flamboyant, always being in harmony with the rest of the landscaping.

A gateway is an opening in a fence or wall, large enough for a person to walk through. Sometimes an open gateway is sufficient without a gate; a gate permits complete closure.

Most formal Japanese gardens of significant size have a front, or main, gate as well as a rear gate used in removing litter from the garden. The main entry is often made up of a smaller gate within a larger one or adjacent to it. The small gate is used by the family for everyday traffic, the large one for guests.

The Japanese use sliding panels as well as hinged doors for gates. There is a great variety of designs possible with either, but hinged arrangements are more familiar—and easier to use —in the West.

When you are planning a fence, have a general idea in mind for the type of gate you expect to construct. The details can change as you develop the idea but strive to keep the gate harmonious with the fence.

The simplest gateway consists of two vertical posts taller than the height of the fence, which form an open pass-through. The posts can be lumber or young tree trunks set in concrete. To stabilize the opening, add a horizontal cross-member to join the posts below their tops, locating it a foot or two above head height. The cross-piece can butt up against the inside surfaces of the posts and be nailed in place or it can pass through the posts and extend out on either side. The latter scheme requires a drill, a sharp chisel, and patience to get the holes in the posts. (It's a good idea to make the holes about 1/4 inch larger than the cross-piece to allow for swelling of the wood in wet weather.)

A rustic fence should have a rustic gateway. Two fairly straight tree trunks can be used for posts (leave the bark on or strip it off), with another trunk—which can be gnarled and twisted—for a cross-piece. The secret to giving a simple gateway an Oriental look is to extend the ends of the cross-member beyond the post and the ends of the post above the cross-member.

The next step to making a gateway picturesque is to add a series of top brackets to support a roof, or add front and back bracing (buttresses).

A gate roof can carry through the theme of the fence, matching board-and-batt or board-and-board construction. Shingles or shakes are quite handsome on a gate roof, and even sheet copper is in keeping with Japanese construction. Thatching and woven reed look good but are not long-lived. You can embellish a roof with a ridgepole made from a plank set on edge, a single bamboo pole or several lengths of bamboo tied together. A ridgepole looks best if it extends out past the ends of a roof.

If you install a lantern or some kind of light fixture in a gate roof during construction, make sure that it illuminates both sides of the gate. Diffuse the light so it won't glare right in your eyes as you approach the gate.

Buttresses, or wings, project out from a gateway, usually on the side away from the garden. They form a right angle with the gate or may angle out slightly. Buttresses provide some support to gate posts but are used mainly for their decorative value. They tend to break up the flat plane created by fence and gate, acting somewhat as sleeve fences, and lead the eye through the gateway.

Buttresses are made by sinking a pair of posts into the ground 3 to 5 feet out from the main gate posts. They can be anywhere from 3 to 6 feet tall, just so they are shorter than the gate it-self. Add rails between gate posts and wing posts (usually the bottom rail is horizontal and the top one slants down from the gateway). Leave just this basic frame or fill in between the rails with boards, grillwork, or stakes to match the fence. Unlike the fence, however, the boarding should be fitted *between* the rails or trimmed even with them rather than extending beyond.

To enhance a gateway, plant shrubs near the sides of the entry and train vines to grow up the posts and along the wings.

The Garden Gate

A gate should be decorative as well as utilitarian. Since an entrance gate is the first thing that visitors encounter, it should be appealing. Gates can be made in the same style as the fence or they can be given more emphasis with different materials. For example, with a board fence you might use a tight grillwork for the gate; with a stake fence you could build the gate with boards arranged in a horizontal or even diagonal pattern.

A gate that is part of a boundary fence should be sturdier in appearance and construction than a gate within the garden. A fence of imposing scale should have a sizeable gateway, which may in turn require a pair of hinged doors rather than a single one. Small openings—3 or 4 feet—are best closed with a single door.

A gate that is part of the garden enclosure should be hinged to swing *into* the garden.

Gates get more use than any part of the garden and if they are expected to last they must be built solidly. It is beyond the scope of this book to go into construction details (see the list of references on page 17), but there are three principal pointers that will help you build a good gate. They all relate to making the gate physically fit the gateway in the beginning and for years to come:

■ A gate must be built true. All corners must be perfectly square and the facing sides parallel. A gate that looks rustic is one thing; a gate that doesn't fit is a sign of faulty construction.

■ A gate must be braced. Whether you use wood braces as part of the framing or a wire-turnbuckle arrangement, good bracing is essential to prevent sagging, dragging, and binding.

■ A gate must be hinged properly. There are many kinds of hinges but the wrong hinge will result in a faulty gate. Check with your lumber man or hardware store for the best kind for your particular situation.

Whatever the type of gate, skimping in any of these three areas will inevitably result in a gate that does not hang straight, is difficult to use, or is an eyesore.

Small gates within the garden are chiefly decorative and can be of light construction. Lattice gates are probably the most common and are seldom taller than eye level.

A gate inside the garden is often left open most of the time to make it look more inviting. Heavy hinges and other hardware are usually not necessary, and frequently a "lifting" type of gate is the most picturesque. This is a gate that is lightly hinged (even cord lashings will suffice), with its outside corner actually resting on the ground or a flat rock. It is lifted slightly to swing it back.

Hinges, Latches, Rattles

Choose the right hinge for your gate. It's a good idea to use a hinge slightly heavier than needed, to allow for wear and tear over the years. For a heavy gate, lag and strap hinges are often a better answer than the more familiar "T" type. Different types of hinges are designed to do different jobs and fit different kinds of gate sidings. Decide on the hinge when you first design the gate rather than wait until you're ready to hang it.

Even the functional hinge can add a decorative touch to a gate. Most hardware stores, and some import stores in the larger cities, carry wrought iron hardware. Look under "Iron Ornamental Work" in the telephone book for places that will make up metal hinges and latches to your exact specifications.

To keep a gate closed, use one of the many styles of latches available or better yet design your own. Most garden gates in Japan are distinguished by a unique latching system which has been made on the spot, usually of wood.

A sliding wooden bolt is fairly easy to make. At it's simplest it consists of a length of 1 x 4 lumber that slides through a slot in the latch edge of the gate into a matching slot in the gate post. Home-made handles and latches for double gates can get more sophisticated and can be a test of the designer's ingenuity and skill. Several photos throughout this book show some possibilities.

You can dress up a gateway by carving your name or street number into one of the posts or, for a less-permanent arrangement, into a board that you can mount at the entrance.

Instead of a doorbell or knocker, tie several short lengths of bamboo to a small board hung on the inside of the gate. Whenever the gate is opened the pieces will rattle. Or hang a set of bamboo wind chimes (sold in Oriental stores and novelty shops), several pieces of metal, or a set of small bells from the cross-tie so the gate hits them when swung open.

NATURAL STONE WALL with large, closely fitted rocks with soil. Some joints have plants; clipped hedge grows at top. Wider walls may have center depression with soil for shrubs.

TEA HOUSE is tucked away, half hidden by plantings, forming a very special retreat for reading or just relaxing. This Western tea house is an authentic copy of one in Japan. (Design, George Kubota.)

Structures and Details

The tea house...linking house to garden with the engawa...water basins...lanterns ...wells...pagodas...bonsai

In the Japanese garden you use stone, plants, and water in various ways and forms that are in agreement with nature and pleasing to man. These three basic elements are put to use in forming larger elements that are common to most Japanese gardens: ponds, streams, waterfalls, rock groupings, paths, hedges. By themselves these three elements, and their many combinations, can be used to create a real Japanese garden or a contemporary garden with just a touch of the Orient. If you use stone, plants, and water in the relationships described earlier, you will capture the essential spirit of a Japanese garden. Nothing else is needed.

However, there are certain other objects that are frequently used in the Japanese garden. They are not essential to fix the spirit of the garden but when used properly they help to intensify it. They do not establish an atmosphere but strengthen what is already there.

Accessories cannot make something out of nothing. As a matter of fact, their greatest value is usually in their absence. If they are misused, they will do more harm to the spirit of the garden than if they were not there at all.

What are the accessories? They are tea houses, arbors, water basins, wells, pagodas, bonsai, and a mixed bag of statuary, stone carvings, and varied objects of Japanese origin. For all of them the rule is the same—better too few than too many; better none than the wrong ones.

There are a few general guides to the use of accessories: First, they should not be placed too close together. A stone lantern, for example, is a strong element. Placing one next to a pagoda— another strong element—will cause both to be weakened. (There are some exceptions, such as a lantern and a water basin, which often work together as a unit.)

Second, too many different types of objects should not be used unless the garden is of considerable size. The more objects you use, the less important they become and the more they detract from the garden.

Third, accessories should be placed so that they appear to *belong*. If there is no practical or esthetic reason for their being where they are, then they shouldn't be there.

How are such ornaments properly used? Study your garden carefully, or study the plans for it if it's in the early stages of design. Block out the important features first, as discussed in the earlier chapters of this book—features such as main rock groupings, paths, streams, plantings. Then if there's an area that somehow seems to be lacking and does not seem to be satisfied by one of those important elements, it *may* be the place for an accessory.

Structures such as a tea house or an arbor must be planned for well in advance. A lantern or a

ADAPTATION OF TEA HOUSE, this garden structure is open for summer sitting. Materials are giant timber bamboo, reed and rush matting, carved panels. (Design, George Kubota.)

. . . ACCESSORIES

well can be worked in as the garden develops. Bronze figures or signposts can be added when a garden is completed, often long after, when you've had a chance to adjust to the garden.

There are some things that do not belong. No matter how cute or quaint they may seem on a nursery shelf, they can only ruin a Japanese garden. These are the plaster elves, ducks, cherubs, and saints. Though they have their place, it isn't in a Japanese garden.

Bronze figures are often used, but only where they fit their surroundings and strengthen the spirit of the garden. A tortoise should be used near water—at the edge of a pond or on a half-submerged rock. A crane may stand in the midst of water lilies. Shrimp, crabs, and lobsters can be located in clear, shallow water where their presence will be subtle. Sometimes a frog can be placed on a rock near water, or at the water's

edge. A bronze insect, such as a dragonfly or mantis, might be placed on a large leaf or made to look as if it were resting on a branch. Tiny deer are sometimes placed in a small glade formed by low branches.

The idea is to locate such animals in their natural surroundings while still acknowledging that they are at best charming eye-catchers. They should establish a bit of humor and fancy without being theatrical or trite.

Metal figures are usually available from Oriental gift shops and import stores.

There are a few other objects that are used in gardens in Japan which are primarily utilitarian but also add a bit of decoration and fit the feeling of the place. The Japanese often tie a 5 or 6-inch cobblestone with rope (much as you would tie a box by running twine over and under, crossing it at the bottom, then bringing it up and around the other sides and knotting it at the top); then they place it in the center of a path. This is called a *sekimori-ishi,* a name that means roughly

WESTERNIZED VERSION of garden structure nevertheless blends well into the Japanese style garden because of good use of unfinished wood. The closed portion at right contains garden storage.

"keeper of the barrier." Its symbolic purpose is to stop anyone from walking beyond that point. The wooden props and crutches used for supporting tree trunks and limbs can become a visual part of a garden. To prepare for winter, particularly in the northernmost parts of Japan where snow and cold are severe, gardeners wrap and tie straw around the trunks of tender trees or put conical hats made of straw on shrubs and even over lanterns and water basins. This gives some protection against freezing and adds a little decorative touch to the garden especially during a harsh period.

WHAT ABOUT A TEA HOUSE?

The classical Japanese tea garden consists of an outer garden designed to prepare visitors spiritually for the tea ceremony, and an inner garden that contains the tea house. The theme of the tea garden is solitude. It is a place of peaceful re-

treat where a person can put aside all cares and spend a few moments examining his innermost thoughts.

The classical tea house, or *cha-seki* (*cha*=tea; *seki*=house), was a place for meditation while sharing in a highly stylized ritual of preparing and partaking of tea. It was little more than a straw hut with an outside waiting area, a tiny anteroom where utensils were washed, and a ceremony room, which was only about 10 feet square. The room was designed to hold no more than five persons at a time. Its furnishings were simple and sparse.

Entry was through a low doorway, so low that guests had to stoop to get through it—a scheme aimed at instilling a sense of humility. Against an outer wall was a rack on which samurai warriors hung their swords, since the tea room was a place of peace.

Adjoining the tea house was a water basin where guests could wash their hands and where water was available for the making of the tea.

Some Planning Guides

The idea of a tea house as a garden structure is adaptable to Western gardens that have a Japanese theme. It can serve as a cozy retreat or as a multi-purpose room. It can be less a place for drinking tea, more a small outdoor room for reading, conversation, or informal entertaining on a limited scale.

The size should be in scale with the rest of the garden. Construction should be simple, materials natural. Use unpainted wood, bamboo, straw, reed, or rushes. Walls can be plastered and painted in subdued earthy colors with a flat finish. The roof can be board, thatch, or shingle. The floor should be wood. It can be left bare or covered with a rug of plain design or the familiar Japanese *tatami* mat.

If you want to retain some tradition, have a *tokonoma*—a recessed portion of the room where you display a painting and a flower arrangement.

It's fairly common to have only two or three sides closed by walls, the others being left open permanently or closed by sliding doors. A single small window will let in light. To retain the natural feeling, the window can be covered with an open lattice of bamboo. The structure should be oriented such that sunlight filters softly into it through foliage rather than shining in harshly.

If you build a tea house for infrequent use during the summer, it can be made very rustic and left open to the weather. For light and heat in the evening use a kerosene lamp and a charcoal-stoked hibachi, both more romantic than practical.

If you want a more substantial place for year around use, you can wire a tea house for electric lights and use an electric heater.

Other Garden Structures

A garden pavilion, gazebo, or arbor differs from a tea house in being primarily a resting place in the garden. The structure is generally open on all sides, with a simple roof (often thatched) supported by corner posts. The floor is earth or rough board. If there is any wall, it usually has a large opening in it—often circular—for light and air circulation.

Structures such as a tea house or arbor should be located to the rear of the garden with a winding path leading to them. Blend them into the landscaping by planting shrubs close to the walls or training vines up the support posts.

There are many modifications that can adapt such structures to Western living habits. They can be given a more practical role by concealing a potting shed or tool storage area. They can serve

HANDSOME FENCE across back of garden marks property boundary. Gate goes nowhere but gives feeling that trees on adjoining lot are really part of garden. (Design, George Kubota.)

More familiar to the Westerner but somewhat less common in Japan is the indoor garden. The Japanese garden usually is thought of as being under the open sky, exposed to the changing seasons. Bringing it entirely inside imposes some size limitations as well as restricting the types of plants that can be used.

Nevertheless, most principles of the Japanese garden can be applied with good effect inside the house. By simulating even a small area of natural scenery you can bring indoors a freshness and naturalness that is not possible with potted plants by themselves.

For maximum effectiveness and ease of care limit the size of the indoor garden. Anything less than about 15 square feet will not be very effective; anything more than about 35 square feet will be difficult to take care of.

Areas near a window but out of direct sun are best, especially if a window extends down to floor level. With plants next to the glass both inside and outside, the indoor garden effectively extends out of doors and both areas blend smoothly.

There are ways of creating a true planting area indoors by constructing a large pan to hold soil—actually a king-sized planter. But such a set-up takes considerable effort and expense and once it's in it's a fairly permanent fixture. A better answer for the small indoor garden is to use container plants and conceal pots with rocks.

PUTTING IN THE GARDEN.   Rather than placing rocks right on the floor, cut a sheet of ³⁄₈-inch exterior grade plywood to the overall size of the garden. (A rectangular shape is handier and easier to use than some exotic free form.) Place several ¹⁄₄-inch wood strips on the floor, then place the plywood on the strips. They keep the garden up off the floor and allow air to circulate. You can edge the plywood with 1 by 4 or 2 by 4-inch stock, stained and varnished and set on edge. This hides the space beneath the platform and it forms a decorative lip to keep gravel in place.

Place single rocks or groups of rocks first, following the suggestions for arranging given in the chapter on stone. Volcanic rock is best for indoor use since it's lightweight and easy to handle. Cover the platform entirely with gravel to serve as earth. You can use dark gravel for most of the area and create a dry stream with lighter-colored gravel.

Decide where you want plants, concealing the containers wherever possible. Shove the gravel aside, put down a metal or plastic top from a coffee can, then a pot saucer, then the container. (The lid keeps moisture off the plywood.) Push the gravel back around the container, mounding it up to help hide the saucer.

Add a small stone or metal lantern, or place a bronze insect on a rock. You could cut lengths of "fishing pole" bamboo and wedge them gently between the garden floor and the ceiling to give the impression of a grove of bamboo. You might also edge the garden with 3- to 6-inch pilings.

Keep things simple, especially in an inside garden. Use a limited number of rocks, and arrange them harmoniously. Limit the numbers of plants as well as the varieties. Don't get carried away in adding figurines and other curios. Don't have everything the same height but use some tall plants as well as some low ones, some big rocks as well as smaller ones.

PLANTS FOR INDOOR GARDENS.   Philodendron, split-leaf philodendron; palm, ferns, dieffenbachia, aspidistra, Hawaiian ti plant, dracaena. You can have bamboo indoors if you keep two containers—one inside, one outside—and rotate them about once a month.

INDOOR-OUTDOOR GARDENS. Left, garden open at end, roofed against rain (Design, R. Kawahara). Center, glass-enclosed court (Liddle & Jones). Right, bedroom garden (Slavsky & Whitaker).

as a changing room near a swimming pool and provide storage for pool equipment.

One homeowner built a minimum structure himself—a three-sided shelter with a peaked, shingled roof that matched the roof over his Japanese gate. The floor is decking over redwood girders, which are bolted to 4 x 4 inch redwood posts set in concrete. The three walls are redwood planks, untreated and left to weather to their own dark color. The only furniture consists of a few plastic-covered cushions and a wooden bench.

Another family had a landscape architect design what they call a garden party room with a Japanese look. Two walls are wood paneled; two are closed with adjustable *shoji* (sliding grillwork doors) whose frames hold insect screening. The floor of the room is covered with hemp squares, except for a sunken firepit that is lined with sheet copper to hold a charcoal brazier. The "teahouse" has electricity, and a small heater helps to take the chill off cool evenings. There is a small deck that holds bonsai and other potted plants and is in good harmony with the rest of the landscaping. It is used as a hideout study and for parties.

THE USEFUL ENGAWA

The *engawa* (a veranda, narrow deck, or corridor) is an essential part of the Japanese house. It serves many purposes, not the least of which is integrating the house and the garden. It is an outdoor wooden platform that extends from the wall line out to the eave line or beyond. It is almost a continuation of the floor, sometimes level with it, sometimes sitting a little lower.

Unlike a deck, the engawa has no rail unless its level is considerably higher than the ground. The depth of an engawa is in proportion to the size of the house; for an average-sized residence, 3 to 5 feet is common.

The engawa serves as an indoor-outdoor corridor linking rooms that open onto it. It often widens to become a real veranda for sitting. In many Japanese homes there is a wide platform by itself or as part of the engawa, called a moon-viewing platform. It is oriented to the east, to the rising full moon.

The engawa is as much a landscaping as an architectural element. Its horizontal plane makes a graceful transition between the floor level of the house and the ground level of the garden. From inside the house it carries the eye out into the garden and invites you to step outdoors.

SNOW-VIEWING LANTERN has broad top to catch falling snow, sits on rock promontory as a light to guide boats at dusk.

SIMPLE, STRAIGHT-SIDED lantern is carved granite, but same style could easily be made in two pieces in cast concrete.

UKUMI STYLE lantern sits on a rock at end of peninsula, where it's reflected in the water. Lantern is cast concrete.

LAMP POST about 7 feet high is wood, bamboo, opaque plastic (windows). Such lamps can be wired for low-voltage light.

One of the numerous Japanese ideas that have taken hold in the United States, the engawa has many uses in the house and in the garden. It acts as a transition that is a part of each, having the structural feeling of the house and the natural feeling of the garden. It is an intermediate step, often linked to the ground with a large flat rock —the shoe stone, where the Japanese take off their shoes before entering the house.

An engawa can serve as a plant stage for bonsai and other container plants. When you place plants on both sides of a large window or sliding glass doors you make the wall seem almost non-existent. An engawa effectively expands indoor space. By carrying the floor line past an outside wall it can make you less aware of a drop-off or steep slope of ground away from the house.

Sometimes the outdoor space an engawa helps to create along a façade needs a substantial roof overhang to match its width. Often an engawa looks good by itself without the parallel line of an overhang.

A Good Remodeling Device

As a remodeling device the engawa is particularly useful for a common problem: how to relate a raised floor to the outdoors. Many modern homes with an on-grade slab floor have little need of an engawa, but the house with crawl space or the hillside house often has one or more places where an engawa can help establish contact with the garden.

This is an element you can add at a cost that is relatively low considering the benefits you derive. It may be a platform entirely independent of the building. Sometimes it can be partly supported on a ledger board attached to the wall. Sometimes it can be hung from rafters or supported on posts that also connect with the rafters.

If you use an engawa at all, use it generously. Its unbroken horizontal line can add strength to a façade too short in relation to its height. It can add shadow line and depth to a flat uninteresting façade. It can support screening outside the wall, or grillwork for privacy.

An engawa can be used on any façade of the house but is most often used in the rear or on sides that face into the garden.

Some Construction Tips

Be sure to check with your municipal building office to find out about any code provision that applies in your neighborhood. If the job of adding an engawa is fairly simple, you may want to do the planning and construction yourself, with the help of some of the publications listed on page 17. If your site is a difficult one or you don't have the time, you may want to engage the services of a contractor.

Unless the structure is a ground-hugging one, the space between earth and deck is usually left open. Many low-level verandas will inhibit the growth of weeds after the ground is once cleared, since there often isn't enough air or sunshine for them to grow. Or you can prevent future weeds by covering the ground with polyethylene sheeting or builder's paper; then cover the paper with gravel.

There are a couple of ways to enhance the appearance of visible engawa support posts. The simplest trick is to mound up a few good-sized cobblestones around the base of each post. This will blend the ground line smoothly into the structure. Another way is even more decorative but must be planned for in the construction. When pouring front-row footings, set a good-sized, thick, flat-topped rock (a foot or so across the top) well into the concrete for each footing, leaving about two-thirds of the rock exposed. Then when you construct the deck, set the posts right on the rocks. For extra insurance against the possibility of the posts slipping, drill matching holes in posts and rocks and insert metal pins.

Planks for an engawa are laid close together and usually run parallel to the wall line. Use 2 x 3, 2 x 4, or 2 x 6-inch lumber. The decking can be treated with a clear resin sealer or stained but shouldn't be painted or the natural appearance of the wood will be lost. (Japanese housewives often use bath water for cleaning the engawa. Over a long period, body oils from the water penetrate the wood and give it a rich luster.)

A veranda several feet above ground may have a balustrade. In Japan this railing is often a work of art itself, with carved posts and wooden panels having perforated designs in the form of birds, dragons, flowers, or bamboo.

In rainy areas an engawa and a generous roof overhang make good partners. To avoid a sheet of water pouring onto the walkway, the engawa edge should stop short of the eaves unless they have a rain gutter.

THE WATER BASIN

The original purpose of the water basin in the Japanese garden was not only to provide a place to wash one's hands but also to encourage a symbolic ritual of cleansing the spirit. Especially in the tea garden, the water basin was a reminder of self-purification before partaking in the tea ceremony. The Japanese never wash directly in the basin; they dip water from it and pour it over their hands, being careful not to let any splash in the basin.

There are two types of water basins used in the Japanese garden, each serving a different purpose, each located in a different place.

The *chozubachi* (literally, hand-water place) is a tall, slender basin used at the edge of an engawa for rinsing the hands .The *tsukubai* (literally, to crouch) is a low water basin used most often in conjunction with a tea house to supply water for the tea ceremony.

Since very few Japanese style gardens in America are in the classical tea garden style, and since not all gardens include an engawa, the water basin has come to be more decorative than functional. As long as a water basin and the accompanying stones that make up the arrangement harmonize with the surroundings, a chozubachi or tsukubai can go almost anywhere in the garden.

Where to Locate a Basin

A basin arrangement looks best in a shaded location against some sort of background rather than out in the middle of an open area. The side of the house, a corner of a fence, a simple sleeve fence, or even a planting of bamboo all make a pleasant backdrop and give the arrangement an intimate feeling. Shade-loving plants or those associated with a damp environment are most often used with basins: fern, mosses, wild ginger, sweet woodruff, lily turf, baby's tears, aspidistra, aralia, plantain lily, podocarpus, dogwood, and the ever-useful bamboos. In general, avoid large-flowering or large-leafed plants, whose dramatic appearance will detract from the basin grouping. Azaleas are good accompaniments if they are not allowed to grow too high, and star jasmine makes an effective planting behind a basin (its flowers are small enough, and the fragrance is an added bonus).

Encourage the growth of moss on a basin by locating it in a shady place and keeping the area damp. This will give the arrangement the cool, refreshing look that is so desirable.

There are many forms of water basins in either the chozubachi or tsukubai type, their shapes varying from that of a flat trough to that of a tall, narrow cylinder. There are square basins, flat basins, cup-shaped basins, even irregular, boulder-shaped basins. The very best, and of course the costliest, are carved from natural stone and imported from Japan. Some nurseries, garden supply centers, or import stores may also have basins cast in concrete, which cost considerably less than the stone ones.

You can cast a basin yourself by building a simple form using wood or large cans. Since the gravel in prepared concrete mix is too large, make up your own mix using small gravel. Or, use soft porous stone and carve a basin with hammer and chisel (protect your eyes). If the stone is too porous to hold water, carve the opening then seal it with a commercial tree-seal preparation.

Water for a Basin

The simplest way to provide water for a basin is to periodically fill it by hand. However, standing water means that the basin will also have to be periodically cleaned or it will become a breeding-ground for mosquitoes. A better answer is to drill a small hole in the bottom of the basin and pipe water in, letting it overflow the rim.

The *kakehi* is a water flume, usually made from bamboo, used to carry water to a basin. See pages 81 and 139 for some of the many interesting forms of the kakehi. Water for a basin can be fresh-running, either trickling out of a flume or piped into the basin whenever you turn a tap, or it can be the same water circulated by a pump.

Water should overflow from the front of a basin. If a basin doesn't have a groove or a depressed edge for overflow, just tip it forward slightly.

The classical arrangement of service stones accompanying a basin is usually adhered to. There is a flat, upright stone to one side, leaning toward the basin, to protect the surrounding area from splashing water; a low flat stone in front of the basin to stand or kneel on; a slightly taller flat stone to the right for setting down the tea kettle or water container; several "water catching stones" (large gravel), which conceal a drain for overflow. Stepping stones should lead right up to a basin grouping. The basic arrangement for a tsukubai basin is described in detail on page 136.

An added ornamentation to a water basin can be provided by laying a couple of lengths of tied bamboo across the back edge to serve as a rest for a water dipper. The dipper can be made from

TINY BRONZE DEER, at left, are pleasant touch in maple-shaded glade (Design, George Kubota). The metal crane, dining on fish among the water lilies, fits in with his environment.

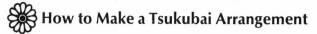
The tsukubai basin is traditionally used in conjunction with the ceremonial tea house. Often, a basin grouping sits a couple of inches below the level of the surrounding garden area so overflow from the basin can be caught in a drainage area and not make a muddy spot.

THE PARTS OF THE GROUPING. The front or standing stone should be flat and about 16 inches in diameter—large enough to allow one to kneel or squat. It should be located in front of the basin, about a foot away.

The setting-down stone is located to the right of the basin (as you face the grouping). It serves as a base for setting down a tea kettle or water pitcher. It should be flat-topped and slightly higher than the front stone. It should be about a foot in diameter and should sit about 6 inches away from the basin but within easy reach of the front stone.

The protection stone sits to the left of the basin, about 10 inches away from it. It can be higher than the basin but shouldn't overpower it either in height or mass. It can be about the same diameter as the setting-down stone. It should lean slightly toward the basin. It prevents the adjacent area from being splashed by spilled water. This stone also provides a place for setting down a small lantern or candle.

These four main stones form a rough circle. Between them are smaller stones that help unify the grouping. The central area between the main stones consists of the sea—large-sized gravel that catches overflow from the basin as well as splashed water.

STEPS IN CONSTRUCTION. Most of the parts of a tsukubai grouping can be handled by one person.

1. Dig out a shallow depression for the sea, approximately 4 inches deep and about 2 feet across.

2. You can install plastic or metal tubing for a system that will recirculate water from the sea (submerge the pump in an open-topped container and hide it with gravel), to the basin, and back to the sea by overflow. With this scheme you needn't line the sea. Otherwise:

3. Set into place a pre-cast sump, as shown in the drawing, and pour a concrete collecting pan. Water for the basin can be piped up through a hole in its bottom or can run into the basin through a bamboo flume.

4. Set the basin firmly in place in the sea, tilting it forward slightly to make sure overflow will run into the sea.

5. Set the other main stones in place in soil outside the sea, then mortar smaller stones in between.

6. When all the concrete is firm, add small pebbles in the sea, and press soil around the larger rocks for plantings.

7. Add ferns, bamboo, or other appropriate plants and encourage the growth of moss by keeping the stones damp.

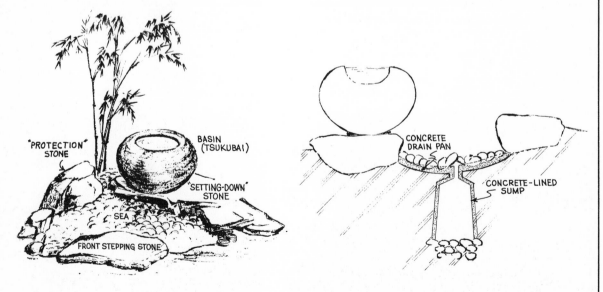

TRADITIONAL ARRANGEMENT of stones making up basin grouping is easy to follow. If you have water running into the basin, be sure to provide good drainage for area, such as foot-deep sump.

TSUKUBAI ARRANGEMENT, at left, has basin sitting in sea; compare stone placements with drawing on facing page. Chozubachi basin (at right) is in traditional location next to engawa.

a 2- or 3-inch length of large-diameter bamboo fitted with a long bamboo handle. The dipper should be placed on the holder so its mouth faces the back edge of the basin.

The Japanese sometimes build a little roofed framework of wood or bamboo over a basin to keep rain and leaves from falling in the water.

A WELL WITH NO WATER

If a well is used in a garden in Japan, it is used with restraint since it is a visually strong element. In a large garden a well helps to establish a mood and also becomes a focal point. Though it may be only ornamental, a well suggests the presence of water.

The average garden in America does not have enough room for an ornamental well, which is usually a blessing since far too many of these structures are made to look so quaint as to invite the tossing-in of pennies and cigarette butts.

More often than not, a well-curb alone will suffice and can frequently introduce the idea of water when there is no other way to suggest it in the garden. A symbolic well can be made simply by arranging rocks in a square or circular border about 1 foot high and 2 or 3 feet across. If the rocks are fitted closely and aren't stacked too high, they will stay in place without mortar. Instead of rocks you can sink a barrel-end into the ground so only part of it shows, or construct an open-ended box using 1 or 2-inch redwood.

Such a well-curb will remain unobtrusive yet

REAR VIEW of tsukubai basin shows detail of simple water flume made with two lengths of bamboo and block of wood. Plumbing is copper tubing inside arrangement. (Design, Shinichi Maesaki.)

. . . WELLS

be picturesque when placed in a setting of shade-loving plants with a few stones: a low, flat rock directly in front for a "standing stone"; a higher rock to one side for a "setting-down stone."

A more elaborate structure can be made by adding a frame to a well-curb to support a pulley. The more ancient looking the pulley is, the better. A length of rope or chain hanging over it and into the curb is sufficient to suggest a means for drawing water, unless you have an old wooden bucket you can set on the side of the curb.

You can use a recirculating pump and plastic-tubing plumbing to add the sight and sound of real water to the illusion. Run clear tubing up one of the well posts, then onto the pulley and down the rope to a bucket suspended above the curb as if it had just been drawn up. Let water trickle into the bucket, then overflow, so it will drip with moisture. Catch the overflow inside the curb in a basin or pan filled with gravel—the pump can be concealed inside the pan.

A well is an architecturally strong element in the garden, especially if it has any height to it. If used at all, it should be used in a subdued, honest manner. Any approach to cuteness can destroy the mood of an otherwise pleasant garden.

LANTERNS IN THE GARDEN

The tomb of an ancient ruler in Kyoto is marked by an unusual tombstone—a stone lantern. The lantern was such a favorite of the wealthy man that his servants carried it back and forth between Kyoto and Edo (ancient Tokyo) many hundreds of miles, so he would always have it near.

The *ishi-doro*, or stone lantern, is one of the most common accessories in the Japanese garden. Stone lanterns were once used in front of temples and shrines for light, then found their way into gardens as a means of lighting the path to the tea house. Today lanterns are used more for their decorative value. During the day they give a subtle human touch to the garden, and at night their light adds a soft warmth.

Whether planning your garden on paper or on location, study the layout carefully to see where a lantern might be used for its practical worth—which is illumination—or where a lantern might round out a scene. Even if you never use a lantern for light, the idea is implicit—an ishi-dori placed next to a path, for example, gives the impression that it's there to light the way. Like so much of the Japanese garden, its charm is mostly in what it stands for, not in what it actually does.

Generally speaking, the best places for a stone

lantern are near shrubbery or rocks that will partially conceal it and thus give more interest. Here are some typical locations: alongside a path, preferably at a turn; adjacent to a water basin, slightly behind and to one side of the setting-down stones; around a pond or an island; on a rock at water's edge; on a "boat-landing" rock that juts out into the water; next to a gateway; next to an engawa.

The following tips will help you choose and use a stone lantern properly:

■ The size of a lantern should be compatible with the size of the garden and its other elements—large garden, large lantern; small garden, small lantern.
■ The form and shape of a lantern should complement other forms around it.
■ The flat side of a lantern should not face the line of vision. When the face of a lantern is turned at a slight angle it is more appealing.
■ A stone lantern should be used in combination with shrubs, trees, rocks, water basins, and fences, but two or more lanterns should not be used close together.

The Stone Lantern

The types and styles of stone lanterns are numerous and the names for them are as poetic as the lanterns are picturesque. There is a milepost type, named after its similarity to the tall, oblong road markers common in ancient Japan. The snow-viewing type has a broad, somewhat flat top to catch falling snow. The dragon-shape type is a ball-like form on a tall stone base supposedly in the form of a dragon's body. Most

stone lanterns available in America are of the squat *ukimi* style, either hexagonal or round, the tall *kasuga* shape, or the *rankei* style, in which the fire box sits on a half-arch that juts up from the ground.

Some of the most charming and rustic lanterns are made merely by placing several rocks of the proper shape and size on top of one another. A single rock with a hole running horizontally through it can serve as the fire box.

Imported lanterns may cost anywhere from $500 to $2,000 depending on whether they are cast in concrete or carved from stone. Locally made concrete lanterns can run from $30 to $150 depending on style and size.

Most stone lanterns consist of several parts which are held together only by their weight (top, umbrella, light box, platform, base). In assembling a lantern you may have to rotate the parts one way or another to get a stable fit. Once you have the lantern fitted together properly, make a small scratch or some other mark on the back so you can easily line up the parts if you ever have to disassemble them.

A lantern should sit straight in its location. Check for vertical alignment by eye, or use a level or plumb bob. If a heavy lantern with legs sinks crookedly into soft ground, make a footing for each leg using flat rocks.

The new look of a lantern will be softened if you rub soil on it and keep it damp for several weeks to encourage the growth of moss. See also page 67 for instructions on cultivating moss.

If you want light from a lantern, use outdoor wiring and a low-wattage bulb, or install low-voltage garden lighting. To soften the glow and

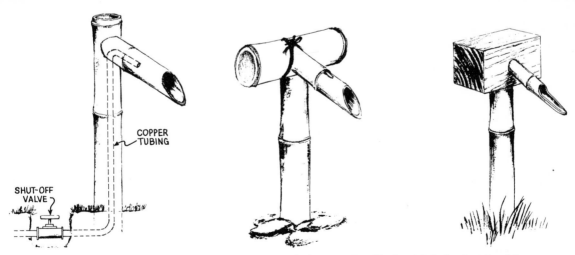

THREE TYPES OF FLUMES, all using bamboo. One on right has wooden block with holes for plumbing and insertion of bamboo. Plumbing can be threaded pipe, but copper tubing is easier to work with.

conceal the bulb, make windows inside the fire-box with rice paper or opaque plastic. For a more natural touch you can use a short candle and shield the flame from wind with plastic, but watch that you don't create a fire hazard.

Metal Lanterns and Lamp Posts

Metal lanterns used outdoors will rust in a short time, but this gives them an aged appearance. Periodically give them a good brushing with a stiff wire brush to clean off loose rust and develop a patina.

A globe-shaped metal lantern or one with a flat round base can be hung on a chain from a tree or from an eave of the house. Metal lanterns with legs look better sitting on a rock or an engawa. Don't suspend a stone lantern—it's made to rest on its base. A lantern with legs should be oriented so that one leg is pointed in the direction of the viewer.

When is a lantern not a lantern? When it's a lamp post. The photo on page 133 shows a typical lamp post, which is a wooden house-like structure with a roof that sits on a post 6 or 7 feet tall. The windows are plastic or frosted glass.

ONE PAGODA TOO MANY

A pagoda resembles a tall stone lantern with several stories of roofs and fire boxes. Garden pagodas range in height from about 2 feet to over 6 feet. These structures were originally Buddhist memorial or relic towers but have come to be used as another decorative element in the garden.

Because of its vertical lines and height, a pagoda is a strong visual element in the garden and thus should be used carefully. Whatever the size of garden, a pagoda should be but a subtle part of it rather than dominating the entire area.

Locate a pagoda to the rear of the garden on higher ground. Another good location is on a small island in a pond (but not dead-center in the pond). Don't let a flat face of the tower be turned toward the main line of view but let an edge be the first angle seen.

A background of vertical lines, such as a bamboo thicket or a grove of birch trees, will emphasize the height of a pagoda but also visually soften it. A tall pagoda—5 feet or more—should be partially concealed by training a branch to reach in front of it. Try to create a view that looks through foliage and past rocks for only an enticing glimpse of the pagoda. This will blend the structure into the garden. Landscape the immediate area with earth mounds, stone arrangements, and shrubbery to give the impression of a distant landscape. The better you can carry through this illusion of distance the more interesting the grouping will be.

A small pagoda can sit on the ground but a large one, weighing over 500 pounds, may require a concrete footing. Just dig a hole about 6 inches deep and a couple of inches wider than the base of the pagoda. Pour concrete in to within an inch of the rim of the hole, float it level with a piece of wood or a trowel, and let the concrete set (if you want a permanent installation, set the base of the pagoda in the concrete while it's still plastic). In a day or two, assemble the pagoda on the footing, getting the individual parts fitted together and straight. Cover the footing and the edge of the base with soil and plant ground cover.

Use candles in a pagoda or wire it for electricity, as with a stone lantern.

 Tips on Using Accessories

Knowing what accessories can be used in the Japanese garden is almost as important as knowing when to use them and when not to use them.
- *Tea House or Arbor.* The bigger the garden the more effective (and less crowded) will be a tea house or arbor. Locate to rear of garden and plant shrubs and vines to blend structure with garden.
- *Water Basin.* Use the tall type (chozubachi) next to engawa or deck; locate the low tsukubai next to tea house or in a corner of garden. Or, use either in any intimate corner.

- *Well.* Locate away from fence and other structures but not dead-center in garden. Shady spots are good.
- *Lantern.* Use at bend in path; next to water basin; at edge of pond; next to gate. Stone lanterns should sit on the ground or on a stone; a metal lantern can sit either place or on an engawa.
- *Pagoda.* Use on mound to rear of garden or on island in a pond.
- *Bonsai.* Use on mound, on large rock, on deck, away from foliage or other plantings.

GRANITE PAGODA is located on tiny island in pond, where height is tempered by horizontal plane of water. Metal owl at top can hold candle. Well curb is granite but could be made with redwood.

BONSAI...A FINAL TOUCH

If you own bonsai—miniature potted trees—you can place a few in the garden as points of interest. Of course, a large collection should be kept in a central area for ease of display and care, but individual plants can periodically be put out into the garden to enhance a selected area.

There are several places where you can display bonsai to an advantage in and around the garden. Place a tall, vertical form on a high mound that will emphasize its height. Place a cascading plant on a rock where the branches can be seen in silhouette. Place a leaning type of tree at eye level, on the ground or on a rock, with a fence or wall as a background. Place flowering or fruiting bonsai where their color will show to its best.

Be sure to locate potted plants so you can give them the daily watering they need. Watch that they'll be protected from direct sun, drying wind, and frosts.

Bonsai should generally be displayed close to eye level or a little below. If you have them much lower, their importance as a container plant will be lost, and they'll appear to be another shrub. *Sunset's* book, *Bonsai,* has detailed suggestions.

A potted plant located on the ground will have to be moved once in a while or its roots will grow through the bottom of the container and into the earth. Some owners have purposely allowed a bonsai to do this, to become in effect an earth-growing tree with a container around part of its trunk. Such a plant will grow faster and be more robust than if it were trained strictly as a bonsai in a pot, but once the roots get going in the ground the plant and pot will be well anchored.

You can grow a pseudo-bonsai by planting a tree or shrub in a section of clay flue tile sunk into the ground. The open-bottom container will confine root growth to straight down and also cause the growth rate to be much slower than it would be if the tree were in open ground. You won't have quite the control you'd have over a plant in a regular container but the plant will develop a much heavier trunk in a shorter period of time. You can train the branches by pruning and wiring to develop an interesting form.

Japanese Ideas that Work Anywhere

How to utilize space and proportion… creating centers of interest … the value of stone, plants, and water

In Japan, gardens have traditionally been designed to gratify the senses and to evoke feelings about man's place in the universe. They are meant to stroll through, to look at, to rest in.

In the United States, a garden must be many things, must serve many purposes. A garden has to provide a visually pleasing setting for the house but it also has to accommodate many pursuits of an active leisure.

Is there a middle ground? Is it possible to mix —in one garden—the American need for physically doing things with the Japanese view of emotionally experiencing things? Can such a mixture be beneficial to one of the cultures, or will it be detrimental to both? What if you like most of the ideas behind a Japanese garden but don't want your own garden to be markedly Oriental? What if you want to adapt, but not adopt? What if you don't want a Japanese garden?

Most of the principles behind Japanese garden design are basically good landscaping practices.

They have taken on a slightly different look from what we in the Western world might immediately recognize just because of the way the Easterner lives and because of the materials he has at hand. Nevertheless, certain of these Oriental principles can solve Occidental problems.

If the Japanese garden designer can make a principle work for him, you can most likely make the same principle work for you. More often than not you can use the principle the way he does, tempering it to suit your particular situation. Here are a few of the things a Japanese designer does that make good landscaping sense in any garden anywhere:

> He practices restraint.
> He avoids clutter.
> He relates house and garden.
> He utilizes texture and form.
> He creates centers of interest.
> He uses small details.
> He stimulates the senses.

CAPTURE THE ESSENCE

Without going all the way with a Japanese garden you can, by remembering its basic principles, capture the spirit of a type of landscaping that has survived as an art for centuries. The Japanese garden respects nature but does not follow nature slavishly. It makes use of man-made objects but in a way that they become an integral part of their surroundings. It is intended to induce a feeling of relaxation, a sense of oneness with the natural world.

There are several characteristics of the Japanese garden that reflect its spirit and on which you can base any garden design:

■ *Simplicity*. Evergreen foliage is used heavily for year-round effect and to give stability. Splashes of color are captured seasonally with spring flowering trees or autumn foliage. Flowers are used sparingly.

JAPANESE IDEAS for streetside planting, entry garden. Left, Aleppo pine, Sprenger asparagus, with gravel (Design, James Hayes). Right, juniper, bamboo, aggregate path (Design, George Kubota).

■ *Balance.* Plants are placed apart so space itself becomes as important an element as mass. Trees and shrubs are pruned to control the space they occupy.

■ *Proportion.* The proportion of all things—stones, leaves, flowers, trees, shrubs, man-made objects—is related so that the garden, no matter how small, becomes a harmonious landscape where nothing is gross.

UTILIZE SPACE, PROPORTION

The sense of space is different for every individual. The cozy feeling of one man's surroundings may stifle another. Space that is completely defined can seem cramped; space that is limitless can seem bare, unfriendly. But space that is only partly closed, that combines open areas with bounded areas, also combines intimacy with a sense of freedom.

This is the thinking behind the Japanese principle of borrowed scenery, a principle that can be put to use in almost any garden.

A garden contains its own corners and retreats. These belong within a garden. But distant and even nearby scenery becomes a part of a garden if you leave open vistas that can "take in" a mountain range, a wooded hillside, or even a view of tall trees down the block. By borrowing scenery around you, you in effect dissolve some of the bounds of your own area.

If the shape of your lot or any area within it is too long or too narrow or too rigidly fixed to be interesting, create new boundaries that destroy the fixed one and give an illusion of greater space.

However, if you have any kind of good view, don't leave it entirely open for a sweeping picture-window appearance. If you do, all attention will be given to the view and your garden will merely be something to look out of. Without actually framing a view between trees—which will confine it—cultivate open-growing trees in the foreground, compact trees in the background.

The idea is to look through open patches of light foliage and look past portions of foliage with more mass. This will tend to draw the distant scenery closer to your garden and also seem to expand the limits of your area.

The materials you use for extending your landscaping should as much as possible match those that are a part of the view. If there is evidence of bold rock forms in the distance, make stone groupings using rocks from the area. If you have a backdrop of mountain greenery, try to incorporate some of the native plant varieties in your garden. The more you can repeat materials, forms, and textures that are part of your surroundings, the more effective will be your utilization of borrowed space.

Space Within the Garden

The principle of using space applies within the garden as well. The Japanese people are past masters at giving meaning and importance to what the Western world would consider "nothing." In all of the visual arts—painting, sculpture, architecture—space has as much meaning to the total composition as the places that are occupied.

In the garden, space is taken up by plants, by water, by stone, by lanterns, wells, and other structures. The more of these space takers there are, the less space there is, and too often the less interesting the garden is.

Don't think of space in the garden as something that has to be filled up. Think of it as an important landscaping element, an element as important to the feeling of the garden as that stone lantern you're so fond of.

Balance open areas against filled areas. Leave breathing room. Temper the physical things you put in the garden with the space around them. A jam-packed garden has the look of a museum basement. Without open space separating them, the physical elements in the garden seem pressed into a dense mass with no real form and little direction. Plantings and structure should be arranged to satisfy the need for the feeling of shelter; but to carry it to the point where it prevents you from walking and relaxing in the garden may result in a cooped-up feeling—the very feeling the small-house dweller comes into the garden to escape.

Remember that space applies to height as well as width. Utilize open spaces and filled spaces above shrubs or low elements by balancing them against taller trees or structures.

Space is plastic, workable, valuable. Don't let it just sit there. Don't fill it up but use it as an important element of landscaping that possesses both mass and form.

The Importance of Good Proportion

Proportion has to do with the relation of parts of the garden, their balance and symmetry. When garden elements are in proper proportion there is good balance and a garden is a comfortable place to be. A garden with awkward proportion somehow doesn't feel right. An observer cannot always say just what it is that makes him uncomfortable in such a garden; it's like wearing a pair of badly fitted glasses.

There are no set rules for obtaining good proportion, which is perhaps just as well since rules

---

✾ How to Make a Small Garden Look Bigger

■ Near house use large-leafed plants, tall shrubs, medium-sized trees; near boundaries of the garden use taller trees planted openly.

■ Prune trees near house to a "see-through" open form. Don't let boundary trees close in on one another.

■ Borrow scenery by keeping open any appealing views of the region surrounding your property.

▣ Use large stone groupings or a large lantern near the house, smaller ones in the background.

■ Create one or two hillocks or mounds within the garden to aid perspective and give the visual impression of more square footage. (However, too many mounds will have the opposite effect of visually shrinking the area.)

■ Design the garden to be on two levels, the lower one farthest from the house.

■ Limit varieties of plants; limit numbers of stone groupings; limit use of accessories.

■ Make paths and streams wind their way through the garden rather than running straight. (Strolling along them, you actually walk farther.)

■ Keep the garden area open by using low, open fencing rather than high, solid types.

often are stultifying. The old manuals on Japanese garden design gave definite instructions for rock arrangements, pond shapes, even stepping stone placement, but designers who used these books were wise enough to realize that rules are at best a general guide. No rule can fit all situations so it should be considered a stimulus rather than a dictum.

The eye is not disturbed by a change if an easily recognizable shape carries through the central theme. A basic theme with variations creates a unified garden with variety and interest, without monotony.

How do you create a basic theme? You must first decide what type of garden you want. Do you want to emphasize the strength and power of rock? Do you want the lush feeling of greenery? Do you want the cool, fresh feeling of water?

Do you want a rustic feeling, or a contemporary feeling? You'll be combining all of these elements in the garden, but which one do you want to predominate?

Once you've decided on the theme of the garden—the feeling you want it to convey—make every effort to retain that feeling. For example, if your aim is a rustic, totally natural garden, don't mix gravel paths with paved areas, lawn, and raised beds. This can be done to some degree in a very large area if it's carried out skillfully. The smaller the garden is, the more straightforward the landscaping must be and so the more recognizable the theme.

How does proportion fit into all this? Without a good relation between parts of a garden there is no real unity and a garden seems to be made up of distinct parts that remain distinct instead of blending harmoniously.

In grouping shape or mass it is easier to gain unity if you join or interlock the units rather

WHITE PEBBLES set in cement symbolize a torrent of water flowing under house. Boulders and ferns make space an interesting area. Note that posts rest on rocks that are embedded in concrete.

ROCKS AND GRAVEL brighten area beneath deck, are separated from paved path by strip of Irish moss. Sheet plastic or builder's felt under gravel will keep weeds down. (Design, F. H. Mick.)

than if you separate them and put them in tension with one another. Portions of a garden can be joined by carrying action lines through them —lines of a path or stream or hedge. An open fence may separate areas within a garden but harmony is maintained if you plant bamboo on both sides of the fence. The fence does its job of setting the areas apart but they are unified by the planting common to both.

One of the most subtle and most important applications of the principle of proportion is that of establishing man's place in the garden. A garden with massive trees, visually strong statuary, or great numbers of large rock groupings tends to dwarf and intimidate a visitor. A garden with gentle touches here and there—the sound of trickling water, so soft you have to really listen to hear it—makes a person feel more at ease. It makes him comfortable with his surroundings, more receptive to sensory impressions.

CREATE CENTERS OF INTEREST

Creating a center of interest is one more way of inviting human participation in the garden. A center of interest is a surprise, a delightful touch that because of its unexpectedness or visual strength attracts attention. A center of interest is important in its own right but it also draws together adjoining areas, helping to unify the entire garden.

The more obvious centers of interest in a Japanese garden are created around man-made objects —a stone lantern, a water basin, a pagoda. Because these objects are different from the basic elements in the garden they attract attention. The point is that although such objects create pleasant interludes in the garden they harmonize so well with their surroundings that they seem less on display and more an essential part.

Is it possible to use this principle by using the idea behind it but without using the Oriental artifacts? It is possible, by utilizing the three basic elements: stone, plants, and water.

Stone as a Center of Interest

Rocks have a way of naturalizing man-made materials and relieving the geometric look that can so easily overpower a garden. There are many ways to use rocks to enhance their inherent nature.

One of the most effective uses of rock in an Oriental way in an American landscape is a Zen type of garden in a lawn area. You use the lawn much as the Japanese garden designer uses a bed of sand to create a "sea," and add one or more groups of rocks as islands. You don't use any other plants or materials in the immediate area but depend on the combination of smooth ground and strong rock to make a striking center of interest. A couple of cautions: It's better to use too few rocks than too many; don't have all the rocks the same size or shape; strive for a good relationship of mass between rock groupings and between individual rocks.

A large boulder is an attention-getter. If you have a natural outcrop in your garden, clear away some of the soil and rubble to expose a large part of the rock mass. Or, have a king-sized rock brought in by professionals. Blend the rock into its surroundings with plantings.

Don't overlook the rich possibilities of gravel for giving an area a light Oriental touch and pulling garden elements together. Use it in various sizes for a mulch around trees, under decks, around paving blocks. Use it for paths and for patio and terrace flooring. Use it in a trench under the eave line to catch eave drip, thus doing away with the need for a rain gutter, or use a small bed of river stones to catch and break the force of water from a downspout.

Gravel keeps down dust and doesn't hold puddles. It prevents rain-splashed mud from marring flowers and leaves or staining house walls.

One homemaker who lives in a rainy area used rock to make a pseudo-dry stream that is both functional and decorative. He dug a shallow trench at the foot of a slope to carry off water that drains from a steep clay bank, directing the trench to meander toward a catch basin. He lined it with smooth river stones, including a few large rocks for variation. In winter and spring water runs in the trench and it's a true stream. When runoff and drainage are complete, there's still the subtle suggestion of water.

Stepping stones and stone steps made from single large rocks are useful for linking areas within the garden. Also, when walking on stepping stones you're almost forced to look at them. Thus they become points of interest.

A stone bench, such as that shown in the photograph on page 28, can be a center of interest, as can a large flat rock located in a shaded corner where it will invite sitting.

Stone is a powerful element. Too much of it can make an area look dry and forbidding. If it is not used properly—the way it occurs in nature—it can look artificial. You needn't create an entire rock garden to benefit from stone; a few well-placed, weathered rocks will set a mood.

Here are a few final hints on using stone in the garden (also see the chapter on stone):

■ Fit rocks to their surroundings. If it's at all possible, use rocks that occur in the area. If you have to bring in rocks, strive for a harmony with the rest of the landscaping in shape, in color, in orientation.
■ Avoid clever rocks—those that resemble animals or other recognizable forms. Such rocks will create a center of interest but they are a parody and detract from the harmony of a garden.
■ Make the most of a rock's personality. If a rock has strong vertical lines, emphasize this character by repeating the lines with fencing, bamboo plantings, vertical tree trunks. Emphasize horizontal lines with low shrubs and horizontally trained branches. Remember that vertical forms are more exciting and lively; horizontal forms are restful and peaceful.
■ Use rounded rocks in preference to rocks with points or sharp edges. Smooth forms convey a feeling of calm; jagged forms induce a feeling of disquiet.

Plants as Focal Points

Some of the big bamboos can take on important jobs in the landscape. Their straight stems give strong vertical lines. They cast shadows only a little less striking than the plants themselves. They are Oriental in feeling like no other plant. The biggest clumping bamboos can provide good overhead shade; the running timber bamboos can be used in groves to give an inviting appearance without obscuring a view.

SIMPLICITY is the keynote in this effective grouping of three massive rocks on the slope of a large mound. Nothing else is needed; the feeling of strength and peacefulness is quite evident.

Certain trees can also be planted close together in groves. Most of the following are bushy when young but can be shaped so that their trunks create a woodsy feeling: Japanese maple, birch, white elder, quaking aspen, silver dollar gum, sycamore, redwood. Many of the pines have a full pyramidal shape when young but can be planted close to make a small forest.

Though color is used sparingly in the Japanese garden it is sometimes used for a strong attention getting accent. It's common to plant an entire bank or a fair-sized hillock with azaleas. When plants are in bloom the area becomes a mass of color that stands out brilliantly from the dark mass of surrounding evergreens.

Plants with big leaves add drama to a garden. They cast interesting shadows and they sound good in the rain.

The following plants have an Oriental look and bold and striking leaves that make them suitable for centers of interest: Japanese aucuba, Japanese aralia, Chinese angelica, ferns, fig, hy-drangea (also has large flowers, so use carefully so as not to overpower area), rhododendron (also has large flowers), rice paper plant, fortnight lily.

See your nurseryman and the *Sunset Western Garden Book* regarding plants suitable for centers of interest.

The Value of Water

Water adds a dimension of freshness to a garden. It has the psychological effect of making you seem cooler and does help to lower the temperature in the immediate area. Still water, as in a pond or pool, gives an area a peaceful feeling; moving water, as in a falls or stream, lends an air of excitement. Even a thin trickle of water down the face of a rock imparts a feeling of activity.

There is something about water that invites you to get close to it, to look at it, listen to it, touch it. It has a life different from that of green plants, perhaps because of its motion.

Even a small pool does not remain perfectly calm. A breeze will ruffle it. A falling leaf will start a circle of ripples. A goldfish will disturb the surface.

The appearance of water changes with the

 Tips on Garden Care

Because of limited use of plant varieties and flowers, the Japanese garden needs comparatively little care, once it is established. The trick is in giving it a little attention fairly often instead of letting it go until things begin to look shabby and overgrown. A sharp pair of good quality pruning shears is the most valuable garden tool you can own. Keep them handy for cutting off dead wood, shaping plant forms, ridding plants of dead leaves or spent flowers.

Instead of planning a certain day of the week or month for a big weeding effort, make it a habit to remove weeds the minute you spot them as you stroll through the garden.

Use a bamboo rake or a broom for cleaning up leaves. Blow leaves away from rock arrangements, around stepping stones, or out of dry streams using a portable blower or jet of water directed close to the ground.

If your garden has an underground sprinkler system, watering is merely a matter of turning on a valve. Rather than lugging a hose around the place, you can set out portable sprinklers, connecting them with hose or plastic pipe buried just under the surface. A canvas soaker or perforated hose can be arranged and left in place, hidden under plants or behind rocks.

During the hot part of summer watch for signs of plants drying out. Since most of the Japanese garden is made up of shade-loving plants, enough water must be provided—by sprinkling or misting as well as deep soaking—to resist evaporation. Use a coarse mulch and water often.

Prepare trees and shrubs for autumn storms by checking stakes and ties. In regions where winter brings snow and zero temperature, some plants need frost protection. Move container plants to a sheltered location. Cover tender plants that are exposed to the sky with evergreen boughs, burlap, or plastic. Guard against freezing of ponds that contain fish. Drain pumps and plumbing.

In spring, repair any damage that may have been done during winter rains or storms. Remove broken branches and clean up trash blown into the garden. Clean pools, streams, and waterfalls and check for cracks before turning the water on.

SPECIAL TOUCHES make the difference. Eight-sided pilings of varying heights were made from square lumber with edges cut flat. Gravel adds interest at base of fence. (Design, Frank C. Shinoda.)

time of day. At various hours it may reflect bright sun, blue sky, white clouds, or mirror dark trees and colorful foliage.

Adding the element of water to a garden is not at all the formidable task many homeowners have been led to believe. A small recirculating pump can be used to make a little stream or waterfall. A special spray head can create a fine mist that will benefit both you and moisture-loving plants by raising the humidity. A pan or container of the simplest sort can easily be sunk into the ground and combined with plantings and rocks to make a pleasant corner.

UTILIZE SPECIAL TOUCHES

"Little things mean a lot," goes the song, and the idea applies as much in landscaping as it does in the area of human relations. A garden doesn't suffer without the little things, but they can make the difference between an artistic bit of landscaping and a garden that reflects the personality of the owner. Some little things may be attractive enough to be centers of interest; others may have a charm so subtle as to make their presence almost unnoticeable but somehow just right.

LOGS ON LOGS, all unpeeled, make substantial fence, at left; stones in concrete blend driveway (Design, George Kubota). Right, support poles alternate with podocarpus at carport end (Design, F. H. Mick).

. . . SPECIAL TOUCHES

The Japanese occasionally set roof tiles vertically into the ground to create various designs for an edging along a path or for a small paved area, covering the space between with sand or small pebbles.

Defined areas of gravel or river stones, as mentioned earlier in this chapter, help to naturalize their surroundings. Around plantings, under decks, at downspouts, in an entryway, around stepping stones, under a short screen fence, along a foundation—all are places that can benefit from the special touch of gravel.

If you're training a supple tree branch to grow down in a low sweep you can hold it down by tying it with wire. But why not add a decorative touch and instead of wire suspend a rock of the

JAPANESE PEASANT gate made of peeled poles and bamboo, thatched with local cattails. The gate leads only into a tangled ravine but it serves as a charming boundary for the garden.

proper weight by rope to pull the branch down to where you want it?

An old piece of driftwood placed in a stream bed (either with or without water) adds a natural touch by looking as if it had been washed downstream. A log just lying on the ground makes a fine bench. Even autumn leaves, left where they've fallen, can make a place seem friendly and inviting.

An interesting gate handle or latch, especially if it's home-made, can express the taste of the owner.

You can make a rain gutter with a length of large-dimension timber bamboo. Saw the piece in half along its length and knock out the inside joints. Fasten the gutter to an eave using hemp rope. Make a downspout by punching out inside joints with a steel rod.

There are innumerable possibilities for little touches in the garden. Those suggested here and those shown in the photographs throughout the book will undoubtedly stimulate you into devising others. Keep the ideas simple—the more involved they are the more they'll detract from their surroundings. Don't use too many of them or they'll become monotonous. And whenever possible, use natural materials in a natural way.

Plans to Get You Started

🌼 A SMALL CITY GARDEN

This small, back-lot garden is a Western adaptation of what you might find in a big Japanese city such as Tokyo or Kyoto.

Enclosed on all sides and accessible only through the house, the garden is completely private—a quiet retreat from a busy street outside. The garden occupies only 750 square feet. The plan shows how it makes economical use of space, a commodity increasingly scarce and expensive in any big city.

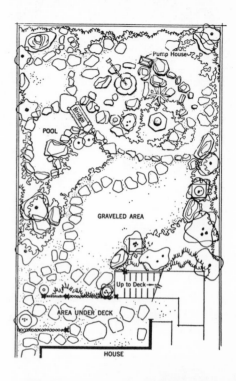

SMALL GARDEN has a unified variety of plant materials and objects; open areas prevent a feeling of being crowded—a necessity in such a small area. Photo gives view of garden from rear deck; stairs connect the two.(Design, Tatsuo Ishimoto.)

🏵 A GARDEN IN THE SUBURBS

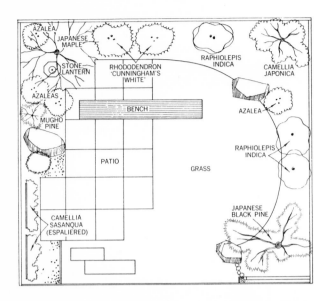

Although predominantly Japanese in feeling, this garden shows a strong Western influence.

In keeping with the Japanese concept of asymmetry, there is a heavier emphasis on design and plants on the left side. Contributing to this emphasis are the greater height of the fence, the dominant foliage mass of the maple, the largest rock, and the stone lantern in the far corner.

A Japanese black pine on the right side partially screens the rear of the garden.

JAPANESE in feeling, but without traditional approach, this garden leaves much of the lot open for Western pursuits of recreation. Plan illustrates simple uncluttered character of garden. All plants, except maple, are evergreen. (Design, Frank C. Shinoda.)

AN INTIMATE SIDE GARDEN

About 15 feet wide and 30 feet long, this garden is located just outside a bedroom. Most of the area can be seen from inside through sliding glass doors which open onto the terrace.

Plantings and rock groupings are kept simple so the garden will have an open feeling. Periodic pruning keeps the trees and shrubs in scale. The use of gravel as a partial ground cover unifies the entire area and also keeps maintenance down.

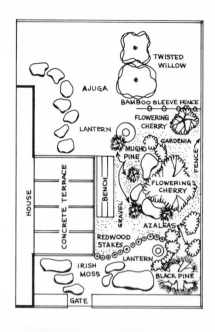

GOOD USE IS MADE of the two stone lanterns: they look right in their location, and they don't make the area seem crowded or closed in. This is a most pleasant place to look into from the bedroom windows. (Design, George Kubota.)

✿ A DRY SAND GARDEN

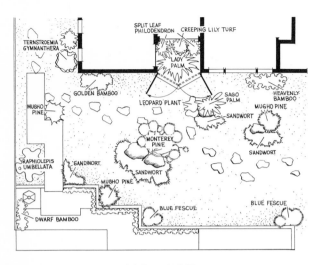

PLAN VIEW

There is a studied formality about this streetside garden. Using only raked sand, boulders, paving, and a few plantings, the garden is quite in harmony with the architecture of the house.

One advantage of a garden like this is that it can be installed almost fully developed. Its precise design, however, requires considerable care. Maintenance of the plant materials is low, but to appear at its best the garden must be kept free of all weeds.

SHADOWS and PLANES add their part to design pattern of this seaside dry sand garden. The house uses shoji-proportioned screens for garage doors and to protect planting well. Festuca is planted between steps and wall. (Design, Chuck Ito.)

A CEREMONIAL TEA GARDEN

This tea garden is constructed in the classical manner, with an outer approach garden and an inner garden containing the tea house and nearby water basin.

All lumber used in the garden—gate, fence, and tea house—is left unpainted to weather to a natural finish.

Note how large rocks are used as accents and as turning points along the paths that link the outer and inner gardens.

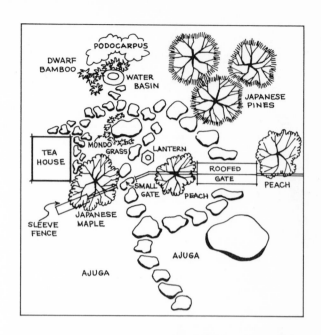

VIEW OF THE GARDEN from the tea house is shown at left. Stepping stones lead out of photo to the water basin; sleeve fence stops almost in mid-garden. Photo at right shows close-up of small gate. (Design, Shinichi Maesaki.)

Index

Numbers in *italic* refer to captions for illustrations.